Praise for *Patent Trolls*

"In *Patent Trolls*, William J. Watkins, Jr. explores the socially unproductive, albeit privately profitable, activities of f   hat produce nothing but litigation. Watkins has ▪   ᴉe and forceful indictment of this expl⌐ᵢ

  —**Roger D. Blair**, Walter   ᵢcs,   Warrington College of B   ᵢ., University of Florida

"In *Patent Trolls*, William Watkins provides a thorough, yet surprisingly concise and readable, description of one of the most serious problems facing technological innovators: patent litigation and patent trolls. Thoroughly researched and documented, this book should be read by all who are concerned about the decline in America's competitiveness in the world market."

  —**Alex Kozinski**, Chief Judge, U.S. Court of Appeals   for the Ninth Circuit

"William Watkins, Jr.'s *Patent Trolls* makes a powerful and urgent case for patent reform. Instead of fostering innovation, the current regime encourages legal artifice and extortion. Watkins's proposals for common sense reforms should be the starting point for this vital national discussion for change."

  —**Philip K. Howard**, Founder and Chairman, Common   Good; author, *The Death of Common Sense* and *Life Without Lawyers: Restoring Responsibility in America*

"Patents are supposed to reward innovators but too often they reward dubious legal innovations and rent-seeking schemes. In the well-written book, *Patent Trolls*, William Watkins examines patent trolls, the laws and practices that give them power, and their effect on innovation. Watkins offers cogent advice on how the trolls may be tamed."

—**Alexander T. Tabarrok**, Associate Professor of
Economics, George Mason University;
co-author, MarginalRevolution.com

"In clear and non-lawyerly language, William Watkins, Jr.'s *Patent Trolls* spells out why patent trollery is so loathed and so lucrative: its rapid rise (with lawsuits quintupling in the past three years), the havoc it's wreaking from Silicon Valley down to your local restaurant and hotel; and the reasons it can be so hard to distinguish trolls from legitimate patent claimants. He lays out remedies worth considering, from keeping patent suits out of the 'renegade jurisdiction' of East Texas unless they truly belong there, to learning from European patent law, to more radical steps like tailoring patent durations to the speed of innovation in given industries."

—**Walter K. Olson**, Senior Fellow, Cato Institute; author,
The Litigation Explosion and *The Rule of Lawyers*;
editor, Overlawyered.com

Also by the Author

JUDICIAL MONARCHS
The Case for Restoring Popular Sovereignty in the United States

RECLAIMING THE AMERICAN REVOLUTION
The Kentucky and Virginia Resolutions and Their Legacy

PATENT TROLLS

PREDATORY LITIGATION
and the
SMOTHERING of INNOVATION

William J. Watkins, Jr.

Foreword by
William F. Shughart II

The INDEPENDENT INSTITUTE

Oakland, California

The Independent Institute
100 Swan Way, Oakland, CA 94621-1428
Telephone: 510-632-1366
Fax: 510-568-6040
Email: info@independent.org
Website: www.independent.org

Cover Design: Denise Tsui
Cover Image: © Paulus NR / 123RF
Interior Design and Composition: Leigh McLellan Design

Library of Congress Cataloging-in-Publication Data

Watkins, William J., Jr., author.
    Patent trolls : predatory litigation and the smothering of innovation /
William J. Watkins, Jr. ; foreword by William F. Shughart II.
        pages cm
    Includes bibliographical references and index.
        ISBN 978-1-59813-170-3 (pbk. : alk. paper)
    1. Patent suits—United States. 2. Patent licenses—Corrupt practices—
United States. 3. Patent laws and legislation—Economic aspects—
    KF3155.W38 2013
    346.7304'86—dc23   2013042008

Contents

Foreword

"INFORMATION WANTS TO BE FREE," a phrase apparently first used in the late 1960s by the founder of the *Whole Earth Catalog*, is a mantra of opponents of tight legal protections for intellectual property (IP). The principal basis for that opinion is that patents, copyrights, and other restrictions on the use of new ideas, new technologies, and new production processes slow down the rates at which innovations diffuse throughout the economy and, hence, impede economic progress.

On the other hand, to paraphrase the late economist Joan Robinson, author of *The Economics of Imperfect Competition*, patents (and copyrights) slow down the diffusion of new ideas for a reason: to ensure there will be more new ideas to diffuse. The argument here is that if new ideas and new products can be copied easily, the economic returns to inventive or creative activities will decline and less effort will be invested both in research leading to the discovery of new knowledge and in the development of that knowledge into commercially viable uses of it.

Trolling for Dollars

Both points of view essentially treat intellectual property as what most economists would call a pure public good. Once a new idea has been discovered and "fixed" in a medium, such as a blueprint, a chemical formula, or a list of instructions to be executed by a computer, then anyone who is trained in the art or science to which the innovation applies can free ride on the inventor's investment of time and money. Not only does free riding lower the returns to successful research and development (R&D) projects, it also chills incentives to engage in R&D more broadly because most scientific research, whether it takes place in someone's garage or in the laboratory of a large commercial enterprise, fails to generate any worthwhile idea or product. Investments in R&D pay off only if the returns to the proverbial home run cover the costs of that project alone plus those of the myriad strikeouts.

Granting inventors a limited monopoly—that is, an exclusive right to commercialize their inventions on their own account or to license others to use them in return for a mutually agreeable royalty payment—has been, for the reasons just stated, an accepted public policy for centuries. Although the term of that monopoly was and is a matter of controversy, the idea is to provide the inventor with adequate time to recover the original investment in R&D plus the expenses of manufacturing and marketing the product to paying customers. If that is not so, the anticipated profitability of the entire sequence of events unravels and less potentially pathbreaking research will be undertaken in the first place.

Given that governments want to encourage invention as a way of promoting economic progress, why are patents under attack nowadays?

First and foremost, patent policy in the United States and elsewhere in the developed world is "one size fits all." If an application for a patent is granted, the patent holder's exclusive right runs for twenty years from the date on which the patent is issued, which is not necessarily the same day that the innovation can start to be exploited commercially.

So, patents for a new chemical entity issued to a scientist working in the lab of a pharmaceutical company, to the writer of a new computer software program or the developer of a new user interface, to the discoverer of a genetically modified disease- or herbicide-resistant food plant, or to the inventor of a new electric or hybrid automobile engine all are granted exclusive rights to their innovations for the same twenty-year term. Technological progress proceeds at very different paces in different industries. The only reason that the terms of all patents are the same is the convenience of the U.S. Patent and Trademark Office's (USPTO's) bureaucrats.

Second, alternative means of protecting innovators' intellectual property rights exist. Applications for patents must disclose all of the information needed for copiers to duplicate an invention once the patent expires and the new knowledge goes into the public domain for anyone to use. But an inventor can choose not to apply for a patent and then, in principle, preserve his or her "trade secret" forever.

"Lead time" over imitators also can protect the intellectual properties of the discoverers of new knowledge. It takes skill to reverse-engineer or to copy an innovative product or process. Moreover, some, perhaps much, manufacturing know-how is tacit and cannot easily be communicated to others in the form of a blueprint, formula, or design concept. A good head start therefore may be all the inventor needs profitably to exploit his or her idea. Imitators incur "first-copy costs." Time, effort, and money must be invested before a knockoff of someone else's idea can be commercialized. And, while the marginal costs of producing the second and subsequent copies usually will be very low, first-copy costs discourage imitators.

The means of capturing the returns to investments that yield new knowledge are not necessarily limited to selling or licensing the products that embody it. In the digital age, the artists, composers, and publishers of musical compositions may not earn much income directly from selling online downloads and physical recordings of their music. But a little piracy of copyrighted material can be a good thing: it generates publicity, name recognition, and, hence, revenue from selling tickets to live performances and from sales of T-shirts, hats, and other branded merchandise at concert venues. College professors who produce lectures for massive open online courses (MOOCs) likewise can benefit indirectly from their creative activities. The business model here seems incomplete because students neither pay fees nor receive academic credit for completing a course.

But the instructor can earn income from students by selling textbooks he or she has written and commends as indispensible for fully understanding lecture material.

It should therefore come as no surprise that patents are thought to be the single most effective protector of intellectual property rights only by the pharmaceutical industry's executives. New drugs, which cannot be marketed unless approved for sale by the U.S. Food and Drug Administration, following prolonged and expensive clinical trials that "prove" the drug's safety and efficacy relative to a placebo, obviously can be reverse-engineered quickly by anyone who has taken a few chemistry courses. For every other industry, trade secrets and lead-time over imitators ranked higher in importance than patents.

Nevertheless, as documented by William Watkins, Jr., in *Patent Trolls*, the USPTO is overwhelmed nowadays by applications for new patents. And so, the default option for today's patent examiners is to approve most applications and to shift the burden of resolving claims of infringement onto old and new patent holders.

Such litigation is arcane, time-consuming, and very expensive. Judges and juries, who usually are amateurs when it comes matters involving technological progress, are called upon to decide whether or not a new idea is, in fact, "novel" (i.e., differs significantly from the prior art of a field), "useful," and "non-obvious" (i.e., is more than a mere tweak of an existing patent). Patent lawsuits consume scarce resources that otherwise could be invested in projects leading to new knowledge and new products and processes. Insofar as it merely transfers wealth between winners and losers, litigation ends up mainly benefiting patent lawyers and the economic experts they hire.

The policy paper you are about to read also identifies another, often hidden cost of today's patent law enforcement regime, namely the activities of so-called patent trolls. The trolls buy patent rights solely with the aim of suing users of the ideas and technologies embodied in previously issued patents. The trolls, who do not exploit intellectual property rights by themselves—they are nonperforming entities (NPEs) in the current jargon—simply sit on the sidelines until a company with deep pockets can be sued for infringing those rights. And, as you will also see, the trolls have found a compliant federal judiciary in the Eastern District of Texas, where jurors reliably return verdicts in favor of plaintiffs and award them multimillion-dollar damage jackpots.

As reported by James Temple of the *San Francisco Chronicle* on August 31, 2013, a study published in 2011 by researchers at Boston University estimates that patent trolls impose $29 billion in direct costs on the private sector every year. In addition to the many concrete (and chilling!) examples Watkins ably summarizes, the *Chronicle* recounts the story of Aaron Bannert, president and CEO of Smart Ride, who developed an application ("app") for smart phones allowing users to track in real time the schedules of San Francisco's municipal busses. Earlier in the year, Mr. Bannert received a FedEx package from a law firm in South Florida threatening to sue Smart Ride for infringing patents on technologies for tracking vehicles and providing users with electronic updates. The law firm offered to withdraw its suit for an amount of money that turned out to be twice Smart Ride's gross revenues in 2012.

Smart Ride likely will be forced out of business. Who knows how many other start-up companies never are launched because their owners fear drawing the attention of patent trolls?

Patent trolls undermine the purposes of the patent laws by adding another substantial cost to the discovery and implementation of new ideas. Those laws, to reiterate, were designed to provide incentives to inventors to invest in the highly uncertain search for the commercially viable products and processes that underpin economic progress. Given that the trolls often target companies in high-tech industries, wherein technological progress is rapid, a twenty-year-long patent right likely is worth much more to the troll than to the original innovator.

William Watkins is exceptionally qualified to write about the constitutional and legal issues at the heart of intellectual property rights and their role in promoting technological progress. An Assistant U.S. Attorney in Greenville, SC, where he prosecutes white-collar criminals, and the author of a 2004 book on the Kentucky and Virginia resolutions, Watkins sees the potential and actual abuses of the patent laws both from the trenches and from the commanding heights of economic and legal analysis.

Perhaps, as some have argued, patents should go the way of the dodo. More practically, patent terms of twenty years ought to be limited to pharmaceuticals and to other industries in which lengthy recovery-of-R&D-investment periods are justified by sound benefit-cost analyses. I have argued elsewhere that antitrust lawsuits by competitors of the targeted firm should be taken with grains of salt. Patent infringement claims by companies who own patent rights but do not use them to manufacture or market the underlying technologies should also be treated with judicial prejudice.

William F. Shughart II, Research Director and Senior Fellow of the Independent Institute, is J. Fish Smith Professor in Public Choice at Utah State University's Jon M. Huntsman School of Business.

1

Recent Trends

THE EASTERN DISTRICT of Texas (U.S. District Court)
is the American mecca of patent litigation. Plaintiffs with no connection
to Texas head to Tyler, Marshall, or Texarkana to file suit. The rules are
plaintiff friendly, the rocket dockets leave the plaintiffs' targets scram-
bling to mount a defense, and the verdicts are Texas-sized. Many of the
plaintiffs holding patents and filing suit are not in the business of producing products or services but rather exist solely to sue. These "patent
trolls" purchase overbroad patents based on dated technology and demand
tribute. If the target does not acquiesce to the troll's demands, expensive
litigation ensues.

Anyone who doubts that trolls stifle innovation need only look at the
example of Brandon Shalton. In the late 1990s, Shalton and a group of
nuns had developed technology that allowed clergymen to record messages that could be quickly digitized and posted on an Internet website. A
number of churches expressed interest in the technology and participated
in a testing program. On the verge of going live with their invention,
Shalton and the nuns learned that a troll held a patent on the process
of transferring audio and video content from a remote network server.
Shalton developed his technology independent of the troll's patent and
questioned the validity of that patent, but he did not have the funds
to take the matter to court. He and the nuns decided to close up shop

rather than risk becoming the target of a rapacious troll. Shalton is but one example of an innovator whose dreams were crushed because of our patent litigation dynamic.

Of course, innovation is the reason that governments grant patent rights. Patents are issued in return for a full disclosure of the underlying technology so that the innovation can enter the public domain quickly and be duplicated when the protection of the patent ends. A patent rewards an inventor with a temporary monopoly on an invention that he or she otherwise might be tempted to keep secret. A definite patent term allows the inventor to fully exploit the market for his or her intellectual property. Without patent protection, inventors may justly fear that others will copy their idea and deprive them of any pecuniary benefit from their work. Society benefits from the new invention as well as the inspiration the invention gives to others to improve it, or to develop alternatives.

Innovation, unfortunately, is now imperiled with recent trends in patent litigation. In too many instances, patents have become tools for litigation rather than mechanisms to create and market new products or processes. Researchers aver that our economy is the real loser in the patent litigation boom with the estimates ranging in the billions of dollars.

This book examines how rural East Texas has become the national hub for patent litigation and how recent trends affect the innovative aspects of the economy. The book begins with a brief historical background about letters patent in the Anglo-American tradition. It then discusses the first patent act in U.S. history and the basics of patent law. Next, the book introduces the emergence of patent trolls, the harm caused by trolls, and recent efforts aimed at curbing the power of the trolls. The focus then shifts to the Eastern District of Texas and the tremendous success that patent plaintiffs have enjoyed there. Finally, the book offers suggestions on how to restore a sense of fairness to American patent litigation. Among the possible reforms are modified venue rules, specialized or professional juries, and the creation of a federal court that handles only patent matters.

A Brief History

Grants of exclusive rights to inventors can be traced back to the late 1400s and the city-state of Venice.[1] In Venice and other medieval cities, guilds developed a respect for what we call today *intellectual property.* The knowledge of how to do something, the guilds believed, was just as valuable—if not more so—than the finished product itself. In enacting an early patent statute, Venice delighted that its citizens had "among us men of great genius, apt to invent and discover ingenious devices" that buttressed the "grandeur and virtue of our city."[2] Venetian rulers believed that "if provision were made for the works and devices discovered by such persons, so that others who may see them could not build them and take the inventor's honor away, more men would then apply their genius, would discover, and would build devices of great utility and benefit to our commonwealth."[3] Accordingly, "every person who shall build any new and ingenious device in this City, not previously made in our Commonwealth, shall give notice of it to the office of our General Welfare Board when it has been reduced to perfection so that it can be used and operated."[4] When this was done it was "forbidden to every other person in any of our territories and towns to make any further device conforming with and similar to said one, without the consent and license of the author, for the term of ten years."[5]

In Anglo-American history, letters patent were associated with the monarch's prerogative powers and often had little to do with innovation. Elizabeth I was notorious for using her authority to grant monopolies via letters patent for such mundane matters as the sale of foodstuffs and playing cards. These patents had nothing to do with creating novel concepts or tools and instead were a mechanism to give economic privileges to the monarch's favorites.

The abuse of letters patent led Parliament to pass the Statute of Monopolies of 1623. The statute forbade monopolies, but it provided an important exception. Under the statute, the "true and first inventor" of a new manufacture was granted the sole making and using of the invention for up to fourteen years.[6] Parliament decided on fourteen years because at least two apprentices could be trained in the new industry during this time. (Customarily, an apprentice served a seven-year term.) Hence, this was the first codified patent law in Anglo-American history.

The United States' first constitution, the Articles of Confederation, featured no national protection of intellectual property. Instead, such matters were left to the thirteen states. This changed with the Constitution of 1787. The Constitution grants to Congress the power "to promote the progress of science and useful arts, by securing for limited times to authors and inventors the exclusive right to their respective writings and discoveries."[7] In his expository writings on the Constitution, Joseph Story observed that for authors and inventors to have any property interest in their works, "it is manifest that the power of protection must be given to, and administered by, the General Government."[8] Otherwise, a "patent, granted by a single State, might be violated with impunity."[9] Story lamented that authors and inventors had often died in poverty and neglect even though the world "derived immense wealth from their labors."[10] A patent for a limited time was a "poor reward" for their spirit of innovation, but Story concluded that this best balanced the interests of the intellectual property holder and society.

Thomas Jefferson, on the other hand, questioned the very idea that inventions could be the property of one person. "Inventions then cannot, in nature, be a subject of property," Jefferson wrote.[11] "Society may give an exclusive right to the profits arising from them, as an encouragement to men to pursue ideas which may produce utility, but this may or may not be done, according to the will and convenience of the society, without claim or complaint from anybody."[12] By law of nature, Jefferson believed, the moment an idea is divulged, "it forces itself into the possession of every one."[13] Ideas were made to spread rapidly across the globe, Jefferson averred, and exist for the betterment of all mankind. Jefferson saw intellectual property as a prime example of a "pure public good."

The U.S. Patent Act of 1790, the first American statute on the topic, provided that a person who has "invented or discovered any useful art, manufacture, engine, machine, or device, or any improvement therein not before known" may apply for a patent.[14] A critical requirement of the application, as set forth in the statute, was a specification or description of the invention. The specifications must enable people of ordinary skill in the art to which the patent pertains to make and use the invention after the patent term expires. The specification must contain a written description of the invention showing that the inventor was in possession of the invention at the time the application was filed. The specification must offer the "best mode" contemplated by the inventor of practicing the invention. If granted a patent, the inventor would enjoy for fourteen years "the sole and exclusive right and liberty of making, constructing, using, and vending to others to be used, the said invention or discovery."[15]

Of course, not all scholars agree that patents properly reward innovation and benefit society. For example, Michael Kremer contends that "patents and copyrights create insufficient incentives for original research because inventors cannot fully capture consumer surplus or spillovers of their ideas to other researchers."[16] Kremer also fears that patents "create static distortions from monopoly pricing and encourage socially wasteful expenditures on reverse engineering to invent around patents."[17] To remedy these perceived flaws in the system, Kremer has suggested that "government could offer to buy out patents at their private value" and thus encourage greater innovation and prevent wasted funds on designing around a patented idea.[18]

2

The U.S. Patent and Trademark Office

WE ARE CURRENTLY governed by the Patent Act of 1952, as amended. The act provides that "whoever invents or discovers any new and useful process, machine, manufacture, or composition of matter, or any new and useful improvement thereof, may obtain a patent. . . ."[1] Like its predecessors, the act recognizes that patent rights do not automatically arise. The inventor must submit an application to the U.S. Patent and Trademark Office (USPTO). Inventors must thoroughly disclose and claim their inventions. If the patent examiners approve an application, a patent is issued and is good for twenty years. (Under prior law, the term was fourteen years. Lobbying by the pharmaceutical industry rightly claimed that fourteen years was not long enough to recover investments in research and development (R&D) owing to the long and expensive process of clinical trials and other requirements needed to secure the Food and Drug Administration's approval.)

Unfortunately, the USPTO has been short of funds and staff. This has led to a less than thorough examination of patent applications in recent decades. Data show that "between 1983 to 2003, the number of patent applications received by the USPTO more than tripled . . . [while] the number of examiners has decreased by 20% over the last four years."[2] It has not been uncommon for 3,000 patent examiners to handle "over 350,000 patent applications annually."[3] These numbers lead to the issuance of "thousands of ambiguous patents" that invite expensive and costly litigation.[4]

A patent holder may exclude other people or entities from making, using, selling, offering to sell, and importing into the United States the patented invention. In other words, the patent provides its holder with exclusive rights in the patented invention. Patent owners typically defend their rights by initiating infringement actions. Under the law, patent holders may file suit in federal district court and ask the court to enjoin the infringer and to award monetary compensation. Infringement is a strict liability tort; that is, relief is available even if the infringers did not act deliberately or even know that the patent existed. The tort system, as a whole, has been moving since the 1960s from punishing negligence and thus deterring future injuries to requiring producers to provide judicially enforced insurance to the general public. In a strict-liability regime, the courts do not ask if due care was used by the defendant but more often focus on how much the injured parties require to make them whole.

In the strict-liability patent regime, patents are presumptively valid, but an accused infringer may assert that the patent is invalid or unenforceable. The losing party may appeal a decision from the district court to the U.S. Court of Appeals for the Federal Circuit.

A company or person accused of infringement might raise a number of defenses. The most common defense is noninfringement; that is, the defendant may argue that its widget or process is not the same as the plaintiff's patented invention. A defendant might also assert that the plaintiff's patent is invalid based on the prior art. Typically, this means asserting that someone else came up with the patented idea first (anticipation) or that the claimed invention was no invention but obvious to anyone skilled in that particular art (obviousness). Another defense raised is inequitable conduct. In essence, this means that the patent holder committed a fraud on the USPTO by not disclosing full information or otherwise being candid when the patent was sought. Defendants can also claim to have an express or implied license from the plaintiff. If the defendant uses the product or process pursuant to a license, there can be no claim for infringement. Under the equitable doctrine of laches, a defendant can claim that the plaintiff delayed filing the lawsuit for an unreasonable length of time and that this delay prejudiced the defendant.

3 | Patent Trolls

THE NORWEGIAN FAIRY tale of Three Billy Goats Gruff brings to mind the troll living under the bridge and attacking any person or thing who dares to cross. This is an accurate image of nonpracticing entities (NPEs), often called patent trolls. The NPEs obtain patents not for the purpose of producing an invention or a technology but to license and enforce the patents. The term *patent troll* was created by Peter Detkin when he was the assistant general counsel for Intel Corporation. According to Detkin, "a patent troll is somebody who tries to make a lot of money off a patent that they are not practicing and have no intention of practicing and in most cases never practiced."[1] Critics point out that "trolls operate under a business model that seriously undermines the policy behind granting patents because they are currently allowed to extract all of the rights from a patent without conferring upon society any of the benefits" relative to expanding the store (or "stock") of knowledge.[2]

Trolls seek broad patents likely to be infringed in a particular industry—they especially like software and related computer technologies. The trolls' attack on tech companies is borne out by the data in Table 1, "Most Pursued Companies," as compiled by Patent Freedom. Not surprisingly, Apple, Hewlett Packard, Samsung, Dell, and Sony round out the top five targets. Patent infringement suits are fairly common among the major information technology (IT) companies.

Table 1. Most Pursued Companies

No.	Company Name	2009	2010	2011	2012	Jun 30, 2013	Total
1	Apple	27	34	42	44	24	171
2	Hewlett Packard	27	37	33	19	21	137
3	Samsung	12	22	43	37	19	133
4	AT&T	17	22	34	24	30	127
5	Dell	28	23	35	19	17	122
6	Sony	24	21	32	23	10	110
7	HTC	12	23	30	24	17	106
8	Verizon	14	17	26	25	23	105
9	LG	12	24	28	25	15	104
10	Google	16	13	37	25	12	103
10	Amazon.com	14	20	38	20	10	102
12	Microsoft	22	12	32	17	7	90
13	BlackBerry	11	13	28	19	16	87
14	Toshiba	16	13	21	15	9	74
15	Sprint Nextel	14	8	19	15	17	73
16	Motorola Mobility	3	8	31	18	10	70
17	Nokia	15	14	24	9	6	68
17	Panasonic	22	13	19	9	5	68
19	Deutsche Telekom	10	9	17	8	19	63
20	Best Buy	14	14	17	9	6	60
21	Cisco	13	15	17	8	6	59
22	Asus Computer International	9	5	19	13	8	54
22	Huawei	2	6	18	13	15	54
24	Motorola Solutions	13	17	10	9	4	53
24	Wal-Mart	5	12	16	11	9	53
26	Acer	10	7	11	16	7	51

Table 1. Most Pursued Companies, *continued*

No.	Company Name	2009	2010	2011	2012	Jun 30, 2013	Total
27	International Business Machines	13	12	10	9	6	50
28	eBay	7	9	15	13	4	48
29	Fujitsu	13	7	11	9	8	48
30	Lenovo	7	10	10	13	7	47

Source: PatentFreedom © 2013. Data captured as of August 6, 2013.

In preparing these data, PatentFreedom has removed administrative duplicates (e.g., consolidations, change in venue, etc.), so that these numbers reflect the actual count of distinct NPE lawsuits, year-by-year.

Trolls also scour the country for older patents on technology that might still be used in various modern products. Favorite haunts of trolls are bankruptcy auctions where patents of failed technology companies are offered for sale. These auctions have allowed many trolls to accumulate massive portfolios. (See Table 2, "NPEs with Largest Patent Holdings," as compiled by Patent Freedom.)

Once in possession of patent rights, trolls lie in wait until an industry is developed and thus has much to lose. The NPE will identify targets, raise the specter of expensive litigation, and then either collect license fees from the target or drag the target into court. Trolls prefer to receive protection money rather than jury verdicts, but they will do whatever is necessary to turn a profit. Thanks to trolls, "the rate of patent lawsuits is rising faster than any other type of litigation" and "Fortune 500 companies are being sued far more frequently by unknown non-product entities."[3] (See Figure 1, "Patent Lawsuits Involving NPEs over Time," as compiled by Patent Freedom.) The results from this targeting are tangible and real. For example, the tech giants Google and Apple in recent years "have spent more on patent litigation and acquisition than on research and development."[4]

Table 2. NPEs with Largest Patent Holdings

Entity	US Patent Publications	Patent Families
Intellectual Ventures	20–25k (Est)	—
Interdigital	3542	1522
Round Rock Research LLC	3539	1222
Rockstar Consortium LLC	3378	2820
Wisconsin Alumni Research Foundation (WARF)	2342	1695
Mosaid Technologies Inc	2023	1176
Acacia Technologies	1786	756
Rambus	1566	682
Tessera Technologies Inc	1324	644
IPG Healthcare 501 Limited	1065	1001
Unwired Planet LLC	1037	906
Walker Digital LLC	890	215
Wi-Lan	864	653
Global OLED Technology LLC	802	752
Commonwealth Scientific and Industrial Research Organisation (CSIRO)	790	598
STC.UNM (aka Science & Technology Corporation @ UNM)	405	293
Scenera Research LLC	355	291
Intertrust Technologies Corp	325	44
Altitude Capital Partners	297	234
Innovative Sonic Ltd	253	180
Interval Licensing LLC	246	119
IpVenture Inc	208	59
Pendrell Corp (fka ICO Global Communications (Holdings) Ltd)	206	35
Cheetah Omni LLC	200	120
Alliacense	198	109

Source: PatentFreedom © 2013. Data captured as of August 6, 2013.

Figure 1. Patent Lawsuits Involving NPEs over Time

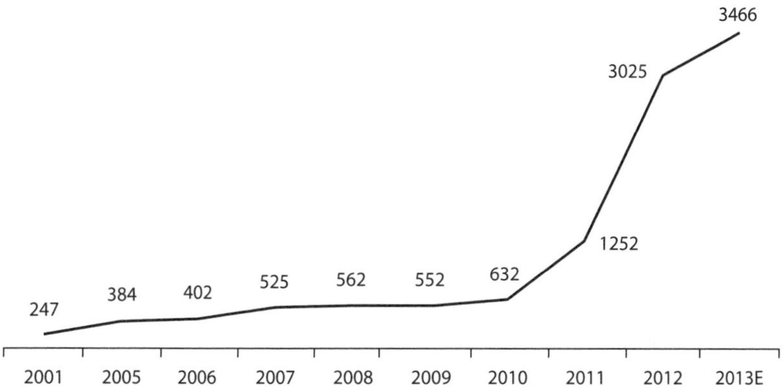

Source: PatentFreedom © 2013. Data captured as of January 18, 2013.

There are undoubtedly a number of causes of the increase in NPE litigation in recent years, including the growth in a secondary market for patents. While our crystal ball is probably no more reliable than others, the continued rise in patents issued by the USPTO over the last few decades suggests that significant levels of patent enforcement by NPEs is likely to continue for the foreseeable future. (Ironically, much of this increase can be attributed to operating companies seeking to build patent portfolios to enable counterclaims against patent assertions from other operating companies.)

Litigation is much easier on trolls than legitimate businesses. If, for example, Microsoft and IBM engaged in patent litigation, each side would have to divert resources from the business and produce thousands of documents in discovery; likely, there would be counterclaims where the defendant went on the offensive to challenge some of the plaintiff's patents. An NPE does not have to divert resources—litigation is one of its central purposes. Because a troll does not actually produce any product pursuant to the patents it holds, this cuts down on the burden of civil discovery and takes away the threat of an infringement counterclaim that could shut down a business.

In the realm of legal fees, NPEs also have an advantage. Defendants in a patent case pay their lawyers by the hour and can expect to expend at least $1 million to take a case to trial. The trolls' lawyers, on the other hand, work for contingency fees. They take a percentage of the recovery from an alleged infringer. Brenda Sandburg reports that lawyers for the patent plaintiff typically claim fees "as high as 45 percent" of the ultimate verdict or settlement, a percentage that is not uncommon in American contingency fee cases.[5] Thus, trolls do not see their money flying out the window with each billable hour.

Typically, in the American legal system, the parties to civil litigation bear their own attorney fees. In patent cases pursuant to statute, the prevailing party may be awarded attorney fees in "exceptional cases."[6] Courts seem to interpret *exceptional* broadly, and trolls prevailing at trial also have a good chance of recouping legal fees. Courts of appeals give the district courts broad discretion in awarding fees, so defendants on the losing end face a difficult challenge if they try to get a fee award reversed.[7]

Supporters of NPEs counter that trolls actually benefit the system because they stand up to large companies that, in the past, could infringe patents without repercussions. An individual inventor or small company, they assert, could not afford to take an infringer to court. Trolls fight for the rights of the little guy. By purchasing the patent, the argument continues, trolls infuse capital into small business that can in turn focus on more R&D. NPEs assume the risk of enforcing patents, and inventors can focus on inventing. No matter how ugly the trolls might look, NPE advocates point out that trolls are legitimate holders of a piece of property and are entitled under the law to protect their property rights. Just as heirs who had no role in creating or building up grandfather's company have a right to manage or sell the company they inherited, so do trolls have a right to license and enforce patents they have acquired.

While recognizing "the theoretical and historical roles NPEs might have played in facilitating markets for technology," researchers at the Boston University School of Law conclude that "the current crop of NPE litigation is responsible for an unprecedented loss of wealth" and stifling of the incentive to innovate.[8] The researchers estimate that "from 1990 through October 2010," NPE lawsuits "are responsible for over half a trillion dollars in lost wealth (in 2010 dollars)."[9] The study measures lost wealth by the decline in company market capitalization caused solely by patent lawsuits. Looking at a narrower window, they conclude that "from 2007 through October 2010, the losses average over $83 billion per year in 2010 dollars, which equals over a quarter of U.S. industrial R&D spending per annum."[10] These figures, however, might be a little low inasmuch as the data analyzed are limited to publicly traded firms.

Trolls claim to be the protector of property rights, but the Boston researchers conclude that NPE suits only "increase the incentive to acquire vague, overreaching patents."[11] Incentives for real technological innovation are reduced. Losses through the litigation "make it more expensive for [tech firms] to continue" R&D and "it also makes them less willing to license new technologies from small inventors."[12] The little guy, rather than being protected by the trolls, is a net loser.

Billionaire Mark Cuban, the owner of the Dallas Mavericks, has become so fed up with patent trolls that he recently created "The Mark Cuban Chair to Eliminate Stupid Patents" at the Electronic Frontier Foundation, a digital civil rights group.[13] When asked why he funded this chair, Cuban bluntly responded, "Because dumbass patents are crushing small business. I have had multiple small companies [that] I am an investor in that have to fight or pay trolls for patents that were patently ridiculous."[14] He further complains that many of the patents held and used by trolls "are merely 'remixes' of early technology."[15] Based on his experience in the tech industry, Cuban believes that "patent trolls are costing taxpayers (via trials/motions/etc.) and small business money that could otherwise be used for innovation and creating jobs."[16] It is "anti-American," he says, "that patents are being held by non-operating companies in hopes that someone will invent something they can sue over."[17]

Some of the boldest trolls masquerade as nonprofit foundations and community do-gooders. One example is East Texas's Stragent LLC, Stragent Foundation, and related holding companies ("Stragent entities"). The board governing Stragent is comprised primarily of intellectual property attorneys.[18] Stragent's announced goal is to provide compassionate charitable services to East Texas,[19] but its real mission is to collect dollars from patent licensing and litigation.[20] According to *Forbes*'s Jeff Roberts, California lawyer Kevin Zilka is the mastermind behind the Stragent entities and "became a leader in the patent game by suing companies that refuse to license a portfolio of patents he acquired from previous owners."[21] The Stragent entities have brought suit in East Texas against a bevy of large corporations such as Intel, Fujitsu, and Chrysler. By casting itself as a local Texas foundation serving the community, Stragent puts itself in a position to curry favor with local juries. For example, the Stragent entities bankrolled a nine-acre dog park in Longview, Texas, and named it the Stragent Dog Park.[22] This local presence also provides insurance against legal reforms that, in the future, could make it more difficult for patent trolls to bring suit in East Texas.

Some trolls are not above donating a patent to charity or assigning income from a patent to a charity.[23] When this happens, the charity is a named plaintiff in the action, and the plaintiffs' attorneys can appeal to the jury's sympathy. Rather than the case being about infringement or the validity of a patent, lawyers can twist matters so that the jury may conclude that ruling for the troll will help charitable causes such as feeding the hungry or assisting abused children. Not many East Texas juries can resist socking it to a big corporation to aid a troll wearing the clothing of a selfless charity.

According to those who closely follow American patent litigation, the Stragent entities are just following the model developed by Raymond Niro, a patent litigator who reportedly has recovered over $800 million in patent cases. Researchers at the Manhattan Institute describe Niro as the mastermind behind patent trolling.[24] A troll colossus associated with Niro is Innovatio IP Ventures, LLC. After acquiring thirty-one patents related to wireless technology in 2011, Innovatio "mailed more than 8,000 letters alleging patent infringement to retail businesses—including hotels, coffee shops, and restaurants—that offered customers Wi-Fi services."[25] Innovatio demanded that each merchant pay them several thousand dollars in licensing fees. Undoubtedly, these demand letters were shocks to small businesses simply offering Wi-Fi to their customers. This also represented a novel and lucrative approach—rather than simply suing large business entities with deep pockets, Innovatio expanded the field of targets and demanded payments that would be but a fraction of what attorney fees would be for each merchant.

In addition to the demand letters, Innovatio also filed over two dozen lawsuits in federal district court. Wireless technology manufacturers countered that Innovatio's actions ran afoul of the Racketeering Influenced and Corrupt Organizations Act ("RICO"), but the judge dismissed most of the manufacturers' claims. The litigation is currently pending.[26]

4

How Trolls Work

TO UNDERSTAND THE problem of trolls, a case study is in order. One of the best examples is *NTP, Inc. v. Research in Motion, Ltd.*[1] NTP owns 25 patents, has no employees, produces nothing but lawsuits, and is operated out of an attorney's home.[2] NTP brought suit against Research in Motion (RIM), arguing that its BlackBerry system infringed some NTP patents. Reports indicate that NTP "had been sitting on its patents for about a decade waiting for companies like RIM to utilize the technology in their patents."[3] NTP claimed that its patented technology provided for the integration of email with RF wireless communications networks so that instead of having to find a telephone jack to connect a laptop to the Internet, people could carry a small wireless device. RIM's Blackberry system "allows out-of-office users to continue to receive and send electronic mail . . . using a small wireless device."[4]

NTP brought suit against RIM in the Eastern District of Virginia. It "alleged that over forty system and method claims from its several patents-in-suit had been infringed by the various configurations of the BlackBerry system."[5] RIM defended the action on the grounds that the patented claims were too obvious to be considered patentable. The case went to trial on fourteen claims, and the jury found for NTP on every issue and awarded $23 million. In its final judgment, the district court granted NTP attorney fees of $4 million, prejudgment interest of $2 million, and $14 million in enhanced damages for willful infringement.

The court also granted a permanent injunction against RIM, which prohibited it from further manufacture, use, importation, or the sale of the BlackBerry system and handheld device. RIM appealed to the federal circuit, and the injunction was stayed pending appeal. The Court of Appeals sided with NTP on most matters and remanded the case back to the district court.

While the appeal and other legal maneuvering were taking place, the USPTO was reexamining NTP's patents. Essentially, the USPTO explored whether the patented process truly met the USPTO's requirements and warranted the issuance of a patent. Ultimately, the USPTO found that all of NTP's patents were invalid. RIM, however, settled with NTP for $612.5 million. This amount apparently reflected licensing fees for past and future use of the NTP technology. By purchasing a license from NTP, RIM was able to keep all BlackBerry devices in service. It avoided the permanent injunction and further delays that would have occurred as NTP challenged the USPTO's invalidity finding. RIM tried to paint the settlement as a success for the company, but the fact remains that a troll forced a productive company to hand over more than half a billion dollars for infringing patents that were ultimately declared invalid.

Another example of troll activity is the experience of Brandon Shalton, who was mentioned briefly in the introduction. In the late 1990s, Shalton developed technology that allowed users to record a message and, within 30 seconds, have that message digitized into a streaming audio format. The message could be posted on a website, where people from around the world could access it. A friend who was about to enter a convent persuaded Shalton to focus this technology on churches, so that a pastor could record an exhortation to believers and have it posted in audio format. Shalton followed this advice and created SpokenMessages .com. "This site would allow pastors to call and make messages available on the church Web site," Shalton said.[6] In 2003, Shalton continued, "we were marketing this service with two nuns on the sales team. We were beta testing with about 20 churches, and ready to go live."[7]

Just before going live, Shalton learned that Acacia Research Corporation held a patent on the process of transferring audio and video content from a remote network server. This was a fundamental aspect of Internet technology, and Shalton believed that the patent claim was untenable. He knew that audio and video files had been placed on websites and downloaded long before Acacia applied for a patent. He also knew that as an NPE, Acacia was in the business of litigation and posed a very real threat.

Shalton did not have the funds to challenge Acacia and did not want to put the churches in a position where they might be parties to a patent infringement suit. Shalton and the nuns decided to give up on developing SpokenMessages.com. In the words of Zachary Roth, "just like that, an innovative, commercially-viable operation, nurtured by an honest, creative, risk-taking entrepreneur—in short, just the kind of project that a well-functioning patent system should encourage and protect—was stopped in its tracks."[8]

Of course, even if Shalton had had the funds to fight Acacia, the law of the federal circuit would have limited his choice of forums for the filing of a declaratory judgment action. Under 28 U.S.C. § 2201, in actual cases or controversies, a federal district court may "declare the rights and other legal relations of any interested party seeking such declaration, [about] whether or not further relief is or could be sought." Such a proceeding is often an effective way to get a binding decision on the crux of a dispute.

For instance, if XYZ Company received a letter from a troll claiming that XYZ's product infringed the troll's patent, XYZ's first inclination might be to ask a federal district court to declare that XYZ had not infringed the patent or, in the alternative, to declare the troll's patent to be invalid. For convenience, XYZ would likely prefer to bring this action in the federal district where XYZ has its corporate headquarters or its main place of business. In addition, the troll has intentionally reached out to XYZ and made allegations and/or demanded a licensing arrangement, so again the federal court nearest to XYZ's headquarters would seem to be the logical place to determine the rights of the parties.

Under Federal Circuit case law, however, the matter is not so easily determined. To determine whether the declaratory judgment action can be filed in XYZ's backyard, the court will ask whether (1) the troll purposefully directed its activities at residents of the forum, (2) the claim arises out of or relates to those activities, and (3) the assertion of personal jurisdiction is reasonable and fair.[9] The Federal Circuit does not allow a district court to consider that XYZ produces thousands of widgets per day in the district that allegedly infringe the troll's patent. The Federal Circuit holds that a demand to adjudicate the parties' rights "neither directly arises out of nor relates to the making, using, offering to sell, selling, or importing of arguably infringing products in the forum, the jurisdiction where suit is brought, but instead arises out of or relates to the activities of the [troll] in enforcing the patent or patents in suit."[10] Nor does the Federal Circuit allow the patent troll's communications directed toward XYZ to count, without much more, as purposefully directed activity. The patent troll, to be subject to jurisdiction, must also have entered into license agreements in the forum, undertaken enforcement actions in the forum, or had some other substantial contact with the forum.

If XYZ is unable to satisfy the personal jurisdiction requirements, it will have to wait for the troll to be the aggressor and bring suit or file the declaratory judgment action in the troll's home district, which is often in East Texas. And, as described in the remainder of this paper, the Eastern District of Texas is the last place an XYZ corporation would want to do battle with a troll. The current state of the Federal Circuit's personal jurisdiction requirements in patent cases puts a company like XYZ at a disadvantage. If a troll is alleging infringement, it is ludicrous not to look at the number of "infringing products" produced in the area where the court sits. By requiring the district courts to ignore the obvious when determining jurisdiction, the Federal Circuit aids and abets the trolls.[11]

5

Taming the Trolls

TO FIGHT BACK against the trolls, some of the key technology companies have formed the Allied Security Trust (AST). Sony, IBM, and Google are among the twenty-six members of AST. Only companies with operating revenues of $500 million or more are eligible for membership in AST. Each member must pay $500,000 to join and then agree to contribute $25 million to be pooled for the purchase of intellectual property. The purpose of AST is to identify and purchase patents to prevent NPEs from acquiring the patents and then extorting money from actual producers of goods and services. AST examines thousands of patents each year and tries to outmaneuver and outbid the trolls.

In 2006, the U.S. Supreme Court curtailed some of the trolls' power in *Ebay Inc. v. Mercexchange, L.L.C.*, 547 U.S. 288 (2006). Prior to this decision, federal courts issued permanent injunctions in patent cases when a plaintiff established infringement and the validity of the patent. Only in exceptional cases did a court decline to issue an injunction. With *Ebay*, the high court held that patent cases are no exception to the traditional framework for the granting of an injunction. "A plaintiff must demonstrate: (1) that it has suffered an irreparable injury; (2) that the remedies available at law, such as monetary damages, are inadequate to compensate for that injury; (3) that, considering the balance of hardships between the plaintiff and defendant, a remedy in equity is warranted; and (4) the public interest would not be disserved by a permanent injunction."[1] Before *Ebay*, it was easy for a patent plaintiff to obtain a court order to permanently shut down an infringer's business. Just the threat of injunctive relief often caused defendants to come to the settlement table.[2] By making it more difficult for courts to award permanent injunctions and to thus close the doors of a defendant's business, *Ebay* has certainly helped to somewhat level the litigation playing field.

The following year, the Supreme Court further gave relief to those companies that have entered into license agreements with an NPE to avoid the risks of full-blown litigation, yet still desire to challenge the validity of the NPE's patent. Prior to *MedImmune v. Genentech,* 549 U.S. 118 (2007), the Federal Circuit held that a patent licensee could not challenge the validity of a patent unless the licensee had stopped paying royalties to the licensor, which would be a breach of contract and put the licensee at risk of losing the license. Licensees taking this path were then exposed to injunctive relief and perhaps treble damages for willful infringement if the patents were found valid. With *MedImmune*, the Supreme Court overruled the Federal Circuit and held that it is not necessary for a licensee to breach or terminate the license agreement to challenge the validity of a patent. Thus, companies that enter into license agreements with trolls have more options when contemplating challenging the validity of questionable patents.

Congress has also stepped in to try to tame the trolls. In September 2011, Congress passed the Leahy-Smith America Invents Act (AIA), which brought a number of changes to the U.S. patent system. Prior to the AIA, it was easy for patent plaintiffs to sue multiple defendants in one lawsuit. Plaintiffs relied on a liberal interpretation Rule 20 of the Federal Rules of Civil Procedure to join in one proceeding defendants who had no relation to each other. Rule 20 provides that one suit is appropriate as to multiple defendants if "any right to relief is asserted against them jointly, severally, or in the alternative with respect to or arising out of the same transaction, occurrence, or series of transactions or occurrences" and "any question of law or fact common to all defendants will arise in the action."[3] Often the only commonality among the defendants was that the plaintiff wanted the defendants' money. Some courts, especially the Eastern District of Texas, folded the inquiry of the first prong of Rule 20 into the second prong's broad wording. Hence, it was easy for a plaintiff to bring one suit in the Eastern District against multiple unrelated entities.

Section 299 of the AIA changed the joinder standard in patent infringement suits. Now, a plaintiff can join multiple defendants in an action only where the claims against the defendants arise out of "the same transaction, occurrence, or series of transactions, or occurrences relating to the making, using, importing into the United States, offering for sale, or selling of the *same accused product or process*" and "questions of fact common to all defendants or counterclaim defendants will arise in the action."[4] This attempts to stop plaintiffs from joining defendants "based solely on allegations that they each have infringed the patent or patents in suit,"[5] which was the interpretation given to the rule by the Eastern District. The House Report on the AIA specifically mentioned the Eastern District and is clear that Congress sought to modify the Eastern District's jurisprudence.[6]

The Federal Circuit Court of Appeals has also made it more difficult for plaintiffs to show willful infringement and thus claim enhanced damages. In the 2007 case of *In re Seagate Technology, L.L.C.*, 497 F.3d 1360 (Fed. Cir. 2007), the *en banc* court created a new test for willful infringement. In abolishing the old duty-of-care standard, the court held that willful infringement requires a showing of "objective recklessness." The court announced a two-step process for determining recklessness. The patent plaintiff must first show by clear and convincing evidence that the infringer acted despite an objectively high likelihood that its actions infringed a valid patent. If the plaintiff can make a showing on the first prong, then the plaintiff must demonstrate that the objectively high risk was either known or should have been known to the infringer.

In June 2013, President Obama spoke out against patent trolls when his Council of Economic Advisors released a report entitled "Patent Assertion and U.S. Innovation." The administration averred that true innovators must be protected from "frivolous litigation" and that only "the highest-quality" patents should be granted by the USPTO.[7] The Report observes that troll "activities hurt firms of all sizes. Although many significant settlements are from large companies, the majority of [troll] suits target small and inventor-driven companies. In addition, [trolls] are increasingly targeting end users of products, including many small businesses."[8] The Report notes that software patents are the most susceptible to abuse "because of the relative novelty of the technology and because it has been difficult to separate the 'function' of the software (e.g., to produce a medical image) from the 'means' by which that function is accomplished."[9] The White House recommended myriad reforms such as granting district courts more authority to sanction trolls for abusive filings, making troll demand letters available to the public, and protecting end users from being dragged into the trolls' litigation maw.

6

The Texas Hot Spot

IF QUERIED ABOUT where most patent litigation occurs, the majority of Americans would undoubtedly answer New York City, the business capital of the United States. Others would point to Washington, DC, home to the USPTO and our seat of government. Another logical guess would be California with its myriad tech companies and research centers. No one but patent lawyers would say Marshall, Texas. But that is the right answer. The Eastern District of Texas leads the United States in the number of patent cases, plaintiffs, and defendants.[1] Just about any way you measure it, the Eastern District is on top.

Looking at the 2011 numbers, James C. Pistorino and Susan J. Crane report that "as an absolute number . . . nearly 24% of all defendants named in patent cases were sued in the Eastern District of Texas."[2] *The New York Times* has observed that patent plaintiffs bringing suit in the Eastern District "win 78 percent of the time, compared with an average of 59 percent nationwide."[3] Over one three-year period, "there were 20 consecutive plaintiff victories without a single defense win in a patent case in the district."[4] The Eastern District is a hot-spot boasting "higher success rates, and larger median damages awards" for plaintiffs.[5] With these numbers, it is little wonder that commentators describe the Eastern District as "the friendliest in the land when it comes to handing down big verdicts in favor of litigious patent holders."[6] Supreme Court Justice Antonin Scalia calls the Eastern District "a renegade jurisdiction."[7]

Not surprisingly, the Eastern District is the favorite destination of patent trolls. From 1995 through 2011, 37.4 percent of all decisions rendered there involved an NPE. The percentage of NPE decisions, the total number of NPE decisions, and the NPE success rate put the Eastern District at the top of the chart for trolls.[8] A number of NPEs claim East Texas as their headquarters and have set up Texas LLCs "in order to better argue that Texas was the right venue for them."[9]

When asked why the Eastern District is a preferred venue, patent plaintiffs cite such factors as speedy trial dockets, judges familiar with patent law, and a neutral venue away from big-city prejudices.

Jury consultants paint a different picture. They point out that the plaintiffs' lawyers thrive when trying complicated cases in front of uneducated juries. In many of the towns and counties from which the Eastern District's jury pool is drawn, "college graduation rates are as low as 15%."[10] Plaintiffs' lawyers also like an older population that is less familiar with technology. Consultants note that "a generally older population of jurors in most East Texas counties means that jurors are coming to technology cases with less experience with complex technology than in other, younger venues."[11] East Texas has very few large corporations based there. "Thus, corporations are likely to be viewed with more suspicion in East Texas than they are in places like New York, Delaware, or even Dallas, just a few hours away from Tyler and other East Texas courthouse locations."[12] Patent trolls can erroneously (but easily) paint themselves as young David going up against the giant corporate Goliaths such as Apple, Microsoft, and Amazon.

East Texas juries also liken patent cases to familiar concepts such as "oil and gas rights or fences around property."[13] This encourages the juror to refrain from engaging in higher forms of analysis when adjudicating a claim. Jury consultants have noted the results of this kind of thinking or lack of thinking:

> Across multiple mock trials, we found that mock jurors tended to think about infringement and invalidity (and sometimes damages)

as part of the same package: In deliberating on one question, they often relied on information pertaining to the others as well. Thus, in considering infringement, some believed that the defendants infringed simply because the patent holder held a valid patent, or was the first to come up with an idea. These basic beliefs often trumped (or took the place of) an infringement analysis involving detailed comparisons of the patent claims with the accused device. When mock jurors relied on the existence of the patent or the primacy of the inventor to support their infringement analysis, the patent holder was given a distinct advantage.[14]

Jurors are not the only ones to blame for the goings-on in East Texas. According to intellectual property writer Joe Mullin, "defendants are very unlikely to win a case on summary judgment, as judges in the district are much more likely to find that it's appropriate for juries to rule on patent issues."[15] Summary judgment is governed by Rule 56 of the Federal Rules of Civil Procedure. At base, if defendants can show that there is no dispute as to the material facts of the case, they can ask the court to apply the law to those undisputed facts and make a ruling. The court then enters judgment as a matter of law (JMOL).

JMOL is the enemy of the plaintiffs' bar. They want cases going to juries when big-dollar verdicts are in play. When flimsy infringement claims, or even parts thereof, are not dismissed on summary judgment, defendants must spend more time and money on trial preparation than they otherwise should have to do. This increases the leverage of tort plaintiffs when pursing settlement negotiations. The Eastern District "has the lowest rate of summary judgment in patent cases by far: less than 10% of all summary judgment motions are granted here, compared to almost 70% in the Northern District of California, 50% in the Central District of California, and about 40% nationwide."[16] A court system that eschews grants of summary judgment puts defendants at a great disadvantage.

Recently, the American Tort Reform Foundation (ATRF) put the Eastern District of Texas on its watch list for "Judicial Hellholes." In its

2011–2012 report, the ATRF noted that it "has rarely found it necessary to shine its spotlight on federal courts."[17] For all its foibles, the federal system is largely bereft of the "home cooking" that occurs in many state jurisdictions, where the trial lawyers and local judges seem to be in league. The ATRF notes that local rules established by former Chief Judge T. John Ward and adhered to by his successors have sped up trials so as to keep defendants off balance throughout the proceedings. Defendants must typically complete discovery within nine months, whereas the amount of time allocated to discovery in other districts is often double this.[18] Trial dates and discovery dates are sacrosanct, with judges granting very few continuances requested by defendants.

General Order No. 09-20 also makes it easy for plaintiffs to judge-shop. In most federal courts, all civil and criminal cases are randomly assigned to judges in the locale. If there are four district judges, a plaintiff has a 25 percent chance of his or her case being assigned to any one of the four. Not so with patent suits in the Eastern District. Until Judge Ward recently retired from the bench, and so long as a plaintiff filed in the Marshall division of the Eastern District, the plaintiff had a 75 percent chance of Judge Ward hearing the case.[19] Similarly, for cases filed in the Tyler division, plaintiffs had a 95 percent chance of drawing Judge Leonard Davis. If those two judges didn't suit, then they could file in the Texarkana division and get a 90 percent chance of landing Judge David Folsom.

Winning a Defense Verdict

While it is a bleak situation for defendants in the Eastern District, it is not impossible for defendants to prevail. To do so, however, they must often go to great lengths. A prime example is a suit brought in 2009 by Eolas Technologies against Google and other entities.[20] The patents at issue dealt with technology allowing a user to use a web browser in a fully interactive environment. The invention, as described in the patent documents, enables a user to view video clips or play games across the

Internet. When in working order, the browser locates a web page, parses the text of the page, and identifies and locates an executable application that automatically enables interactive viewing of the object. In essence, Eolas claims to have created the first web browser that supported plugins. The interactive Web, Eolas says, is its invention.

In 2009, an Illinois jury in a similar case brought by Eolas against Microsoft returned a $520 million verdict for Eolas. The parties to the Illinois matter eventually settled the case for a lesser amount. But the victory in the land of Lincoln led to the suit against Google and others in Texas.

During the course of the Texas litigation, various defendants settled with Eolas rather than risk being on the losing end of another Microsoft verdict. Only Google, Yahoo, Amazon, and J. C. Penney hung in through the final verdict. The defense called on Tim Berners-Lee, who is the inventor of the World Wide Web, to testify. Berners-Lee teaches at MIT and had never before testified in a courtroom. When asked why he never sought a patent on the World Wide Web, Berners-Lee responded that "the internet was already around. I was taking hypertext, and it was around a long time too. I was taking stuff we knew how to do . . . . All I was doing was putting together bits that had been around for years in a particular combination to meet the needs that I have."[21] Berners-Lee told the jury that "we all own" the Web and that it is interactive. He also showed the jury correspondence dating back to 1991 to establish that Eolas's "invention" had been around long before anyone sought a patent.

After hearing from the father of the Web, the jury found for the defendants. Eolas asked for a new trial, but Judge Davis denied the motion. If Berners-Lee had not been persuaded that the Web was at stake and that he had to get involved in this fight, patent troll Eloas might have scored another huge payday. Fortunately, the defense lawyers brought in a tech legend to ensure that the Web remains open with easy access for all.

7

Learning from the Texas Docket

OF COURSE, NOT only patent trolls love the Eastern District; all patent plaintiffs do. Although only about 5 percent of patent cases ever go to trial, when they do, there is typically a multimillion-dollar payday. The following surveys the types of cases brought in the Eastern District—by both NPEs and practicing entities—and the plaintiff-friendly outcomes. These cases were pulled from the Eastern District's docket and are meant to give the reader a glimpse of what the courts' dockets look like. The claims and defenses are couched in legalese, but the ultimate stake is easy to understand: enormous streams of revenue. Readers should note the frequency with which the plaintiff sues multiple, unrelated defendants and the fact that many defendants settle and make payments to the plaintiff rather than risking a Texas-sized outcome.

Imonex Services Inc. v. W. H. Munzprufer: $10.3 million verdict

In March 2002, Imonex brought a patent infringement suit against W. H. Munzprufer.[1] The patents in issue were for coin selectors. Imonex's technology differentiates between coins of different diameters. In the machines, a coin enters the selector at the top of a vertical coin race. This race holds the coin on edge. A protrusion on one side wall of the race deflects the coin toward an opening on the opposite wall. If the coin's diameter is equal to or smaller than the opening, it falls through; otherwise it continues down the race. Machines made by the defendant, Imonex contended, impermissibly used patented technology. The case was assigned to Judge John T. Ward. A jury decided that Imonex's patents were valid, enforceable, and willfully infringed and awarded damages of $10,350,000 to Imonex. The district court, however, found that the jury had not heard a sufficient evidence on damages and ordered a second trial on that issue. The second jury awarded damages of $1,396,872 to Imonex. The district court also awarded attorney fees to Imonex. This award was upheld on appeal.

Halliburton Energy Servs. v. Smith Int'l: $24 million verdict

In September 2002, Halliburton sued Smith for patent infringement.[2] This action involved Smith's alleged infringement of Halliburton's patents relating to drill bits and methods of designing drill bits used in oil and gas recovery operations. Halliburton's claimed innovation was an improvement on methods of designing roller cone bits and the bits themselves by balancing both the force exerted on each of the cones (force balancing) and the amount of volume each cone removes (volume balancing). Halliburton argued that Smith used this force and volume balancing technology when making drill bits. The case was assigned to Judge Leonard Davis and went to trial in July 2004. The jury found that Smith had infringed the patents and that the infringement was willful. The jury awarded $24 million in actual damages. The court added $12 million for willful infringement, $4 million in attorney fees, and $972,386.00 in prejudgment interest.

Visto Corp. v. Seven Networks, Inc.: $3.6 million verdict

In September 2003, Visto sued Seven Networks for patent infringement.[3] According to the complaint, Visto is a "provider of personal and corporate wireless messaging solutions to mobile operators for personal and corporate use."[4] Visto's technology provides secure access for corporate messaging applications over networks and on a broad array of devices such as PDAs and smartphones. Seven Networks provides messaging products and services that Visto claimed infringed its patented technology permitting mobile phone users to download emails. The case was assigned to Judge John Ward and went to trial in April 2006. The jury found for Visto and rendered a $3.6 million verdict. The court doubled this amount because of a willful infringement finding. The court also awarded Visto prejudgment interest, attorney fees, and a permanent injunction.

TiVo, Inc. v. EchoStar Communications Corp: $73.9 million verdict

In January 2004, TiVo brought a patent infringement suit against EchoStar.[5] TiVo's patents dealt with a technology that enables television users to "time-shift" television signals, that is, to record a television program in digital format and to replay, pause, fast forward, or reverse while the program is playing on the user's television set. The technology enables time shifting both for previously recorded programs and for programs that are currently being recorded. EchoStar made digital video recorders (DVRs), which TiVo claimed infringed on the patents. The case was assigned to Judge David Folsom and went to trial in April 2006. At the conclusion of the trial, the jury found that the DVRs literally infringed the asserted hardware and software claims. The jury awarded TiVo a total of $73,991,964 in damages ($32,663,906 in lost profits and $41,328,058 in reasonable royalties). The district court entered judgment on the verdict and issued a permanent injunction against EchoStar. The case was eventually settled for $500 million and an agreement by TiVo to license its technology to EchoStar entities.

Paice LLC v. Toyota Motor Corp.: $4.2 million verdict

In June 2004, Paice sued Toyota for patent infringement.[6] The patents at issue related to drive trains for hybrid electric vehicles. Paice claimed that Toyota was infringing its patents dealing with a method for supplying power from an electric motor and an internal combustion engine. The case was assigned to Judge David Folsom and went to trial in December 2005. The jury found for Paice and awarded $4.2 million in damages. In its final judgment, the court awarded prejudgment interest and an ongoing royalty for the life of one of the patents.

Z4 Technologies Inc. v. Microsoft Corp.: $115 million verdict

In September 2004, z4 Technologies sued the technology companies Microsoft and Autodesk (a maker of 3D design software).[7] Plaintiff z4 is the assignee of two patents related to the prevention of software piracy. The patents are directed specifically to the problem of "illicit copying and unauthorized use" of computer software. The invention controls the number of copies of authorized software by monitoring registration information and by requiring authorized users periodically to update a password or authorization code provided by a password administrator. The patents disclosed a multistep user authorization scheme whereby an initial password or authorization code grants the user a grace period for a fixed number of uses or period of time. Users must then submit registration information to a representative of the software developer to receive a second password or authorization code, which is required to enable the product for use beyond this grace period.

In the litigation, z4 alleged that Microsoft's Product Activation feature, as implemented in its Office suite of software applications and its Windows operating system, infringed each of the asserted claims. Microsoft countered that it did not infringe z4's patents, and that an invention asking users to input two passwords during the process of activating newly installed software with the aim of deterring piracy was open and obvious and not subject to patentability. The jury awarded $115 million against Microsoft, and the district court added on $25 million for willful infringement. The district court also awarded z4 attorney fees. Autodesk was ordered to pay $18 million. The case was appealed to the Federal Circuit and affirmed.

Finisar Corp. v. DirectTV Group Inc.: $78.9 million verdict

In April 2005, Finisar brought suit against DirectTV.[8] The patent in question outlines systems and methods for scheduling transmission of database tiers upon specific demand or at specific times and rates of repetition. The patent describes an information broadcasting system that gives subscribers access to video and audio programs through high-speed satellite or cable links. The case was assigned to Judge Ron Clark and went to trial in June 2006. Finisar was awarded $78.9 million by the jury with an additional $25 million awarded for willful infringement, plus back interest and an ongoing royalty stream. DirectTV appealed the jury's verdict to the Federal Circuit. The Federal Circuit overturned the award of damages. The appellate court held that the infringement judgment could not survive because Finisar's infringement case relied on the district court's erroneous interpretation of a "vital term" in the patent. The court also reversed the finding on direct infringement.

Orion IP, LLC v. Hyundai Motor America, Inc.: $34 million verdict

In August 2005, Orion sued Hyundai and twenty other automakers, alleging that their online sales systems infringed certain patents.[9] The patents involve a method for assisting a salesperson in selecting parts corresponding to a customer's need by using a computerized inventory system. Orion claims the invention eliminated the need for salespersons to use paper catalogs and order forms. Another patent asserts creation of a system that allows a salesperson to conduct an electronic search to determine whether the appropriate part is available and how much it costs. In other words, Orion claimed to hold a patent for an electronic parts catalog. Hyundai argued that electronic parts catalogs existed and were in use long before the patents at issue had been granted. The case was assigned to Judge Leonard Davis. Orion settled with all defendants, except for Hyundai, prior to the trial. The jury found that Hyundai infringed one of the patents and awarded $34 million. The district court denied Hyundai's post-verdict motions for relief, and the case was appealed to the Federal Circuit. The Federal Circuit reversed on the grounds that Orion's patent was invalid because it had been anticipated by a promotional brochure for an electronics part catalog. The brochure was published and circulated in 1987, one year before Orion's claimed patent. Accordingly, the $34 million award was vacated.

DDR Holdings, LLC v. Hotels.com: $1.5 million verdict

In January 2006, DDR Holdings brought suit against Hotels.com and other similar companies operating in the online travel reservations sector.[10] DDR alleged infringement of several patents related to e-commerce outsourcing. DDR contended that such patents may be infringed when an ordering website serves up order pages that have the "look and feel" of referring websites, such that consumers are unaware that they have navigated away from the referring website to the ordering website. So, if a website has the look and feel of the host site, DDR claimed that its patent had been infringed. The case was assigned to Judge Rodney Gilstrap. DDR settled with most of the defendants, but Digital River and World Travel Holdings went to trial. Digital River argued that its e-commerce business predated the existence of the relevant patents by two years and that throughout its history, it had enabled ordering sites to look and feel like the host site. The jury found for the plaintiff and awarded DDR $1.5 million in damages.

Mirror Worlds, LLC v. Apple: $208.5 million verdict

In March 2008, Mirror Worlds brought suit against Apple. The patents at issue shared a common description and are generally directed to searching, displaying, and archiving computer files.[11] According to the patent specifications, Mirror Worlds owned a "document streaming" operating system that identifies documents with a time stamp instead of a file name and maintains them in chronologically ordered streams. The documents in the stream can consist of pictures, text, movies, and any other type of data. By tracking of all the documents on the computer in chronologically ordered streams and making the location and nature of file storage transparent to the user, the invention purportedly improves filing operations and enhances the quality of the user's experience. The patents describe displaying the stream as stacked images that appear to be receding and foreshortened. Mirror Worlds charged that all Apple computers and servers that run certain Mac OS X operating systems were infringing on the patent. Specifically, Mirror Worlds complained about the Apple operating system's indexing applications, a graphical user interface that allows a user to flip through a stack of documents, and an automatic archiving and back-up application.

The case was assigned to Judge Leonard Davis and went to trial in September 2010. The jury returned a verdict in favor of Mirror Worlds and awarded $208.5 million in damages. In separate rulings—one after Mirror Worlds presented its case and another after the jury verdict—the district court entered judgment in Apple's favor, finding that Apple was not liable as a matter of law for infringement of any of the asserted patent claims and vacating the damages verdict. Judge Davis ruled that because the Apple computers did not automatically perform the ordering and sorting of documents but rather required user interface, direct infringement could not be proven. The judge also rejected the damages calculation Mirror Worlds had presented to the jury because Apple would never have paid such a high royalty rate for an isolated feature in its complex product. While the entry of JMOL was a positive, one wonders why the court allowed the case to go to the jury at all when, at least by the close of the plaintiff's case, the court had all information needed to render JMOL.

Cardsoft Inc. v. Verifone Inc.: $15.4 million verdict

In March 2008, Cardsoft brought suit against Verifone and other defendants manufacturing electronic point-of-sale systems (e.g., the machines where a shopper swipes his credit card at the grocery store).[12] The patents at issue are directed to preparing and processing information to be communicated via a network or from other data carriers. Cardsoft alleged that defendants used its point-of-sale technology in manufacturing machines. The case was assigned to Magistrate Judge Roy Payne and went to trial in June 2012. Multiple defendants settled with Cardsoft prior to trial. The jury found in favor of Ingenico SA, but hit VeriFone and another defendant with $15.4 million in damages.

SSL Services, LLC v. Citrix Sys. Inc.: $10 million verdict

In June 2008, SSL Services sued Citrix for allegedly infringing patents relating to virtual private network (VPN) technology.[13] According to the complaint, "a VPN is a private communications network to communicate confidentially over a public network (e.g., the Internet)."[14] Citrix provides Internet-based products that allow consumers and businesses to remotely access computer systems from Web browsers. Citrix calls this type of technology its GoTo Products. SSL claimed that the GoTo Products were an infringement of its networking patents. Citrix countered that the technology in GoTo Products utilized a method of sending information that differed from what was covered by the SSL patents. The case was originally assigned to Judge John T. Ward and later reassigned to Judge Rodney Gilstrap. The case went to trial in June 2012, and a jury returned a $10 million verdict in favor of SSL. The jury concluded that Citrix infringed only one of the patents at issue. Judge Gilstrap ordered that Citrix pay an additional $5 million to SSL for willful infringement.[15]

Fractus, S.A., v. Samsung Electronics Co.: $23 million verdict

In May 2009, Fractus brought a patent infringement suit against Samsung and other cell phone manufacturers.[16] Fractus is based in Spain and holds the rights to several U.S. patents concerning cell phone antenna technology. Specifically, Fractus's claim involves a geometric design of antennas with two main advantages: multiband operation and/or small size. Fractus alleged that various cell phone models contained infringing internal multiband antennas. The suit was filed in the Tyler Division and assigned to Judge Leonard Davis. Many defendants, including Sharp Corporation and Palm, Inc., settled with Fractus for nearly $70 million in patent license fees.[17] Samsung proceeded to trial, and the jury took only two hours to return a $23 million verdict. Fractus had asked for a royalty of 1 cent per phone manufactured, but the jury awarded 35 cents per phone. Judge Davis awarded Fractus an additional $15 million in enhanced damages for Samsung's willful infringement of the patents.[18] The court denied Fractus's request for a permanent injunction because it did not appear that Fractus was still manufacturing cell phone antennas and because Samsung was not in direct competition with Fractus inasmuch as it sells phones and not antennas.[19]

Cheetah Omni LLC v. Verizon Communications: **$5.4 million verdict**

In June 2009, Cheetah Omni brought an infringement action against Verizon Communications and Grande Communications Networks.[20] The patents at issue covered optical processing systems used to transmit television, Internet, and phone service using fiber optics connected to a customer's dwelling. This "fiber to the home" technology permits delivery of large quantities of information at high speeds. Cheetah alleged that Verizon's fiber optic service infringed the patents. Verizon has deployed this network service in the northeastern United States, Texas, and Southern California. The case was assigned to Judge Leonard Davis. Grande Communication settled with Cheetah Omni prior to the case going to trial in March 2011. The jury returned a verdict of $5.4 million in damages against Verizon.

Soverain Software LLC v. J. C. Penney Co.: **$18 million verdict**

In June 2009, Soverain brought suit against J. C. Penney Co. and more than dozen companies.[21] Soverain's patents are for software used to conduct e-commerce transactions. Generally, they purport to cover the performance of electronic commerce transactions over the Internet—especially those using shopping cart features and online billing statements. The case was assigned to Judge Leonard Davis and went to trial in November 2011. Most of the defendants settled prior to trial. The jury awarded Soverain $18 million from Avon Products Inc. and Victoria's Secret.

Clear with Computers, LLC v. Hyundai Motor America, Inc.: **$11.6 million verdict**

In October 2009, Clear with Computers sued Hyundai.[22] The patent at issue is called an electronic proposal preparation system, described as an electronic system for creating customized product proposals that stores pictures and text segments to be used as building blocks in creating the proposal. Clear with Computers contended that Hyundai's website infringed on its patents by incorporating various supply chain methods, sales methods, sales systems, marketing methods, marketing systems, and inventory systems. Hyundai argued that it did not infringe because some of the allegedly infringing actions are performed by the computers of users who log on to the site in question and other allegedly infringing actions are performed by third-party Web providers that Hyundai does not control. The case was assigned to Judge Leonard Davis. In June 2011 the case went to trial. The jury found for Clear with Computers and awarded it $11.6 million.

Internet Machines LLC v. Alienware Corp.: $1 million verdict

In February 2010, Internet Machines LLC sued Alienware Corporation and eighteen other defendants.[23] The patents at issue concerned devices that route or "switch" data inside a computer. Obviously, data must be able to move between internal components to carry out a computer's operations. Switches connect two or more devices in the computer. Internet Machines alleged that defendant electronics makers violated its patents when building certain high-speed computer expansion card connections. The case was assigned to Judge Michael H. Schneider. In February 2012, the case went to trial against six of the defendants. The jury found that all of Internet Machines' claims on the patents were valid and that the defendants had willfully violated them by selling certain devices. The award was $1 million.

VirnetX, Inc. v. Cisco Systems, Inc.: $368 million verdict

In August 2010, VirnetX brought suit against Cisco Systems, Apple, and several other technology companies.[24] The patents at issue covered a method of transparently creating a virtual private network (VPN) between a client computer and a target computer, methods for establishing a VPN without requiring the user to enter user identification information, and methods for establishing a VPN using a secure domain service. VirnetX claimed that Apple's FaceTime function used on the iPhone, iPod Touch, and iPad infringed the patents. At base, FaceTime allows Mac computer users to make video calls to an iPhone, iPod Touch, or iPad. Apple contended that if the patents were implicated at all, only a minuscule part of the VirnetX technology went into the Apple devices. Judge Leonard Davis was assigned to the case. The November 2012 trial proceeded against only Apple. The jury found for VirnetX and awarded $368,160,000 in damages. In May 2010, VirnetX settled a similar case against Microsoft. According to the known provisions of the settlement, Microsoft agreed to pay $200 million and become a VirnetX licensee.

The above is just a taste of what the results are when trolls and patent plaintiffs head for the Lone Star State. The real casualty count is found not in the jury verdicts, but in the myriad unreported settlements where innovative companies pay out millions to avoid litigating in an arena where the deck is stacked against them.

Common themes run through these cases. First, we see multiple defendants being sued when the only real commonality is that they are all targets of a single plaintiff. The AIA promises reforms in this area, but there is always a danger that inventive judicial interpretations will weaken Congress's efforts to enact stricter joinder provisions. Another commonality is the nature of the cases. Most of the cases described above deal with software or related technology. Such matters are often beyond the kens of lay jurors and are susceptible to older and overly broad patent claims. The reader will also notice how quickly these cases proceed to trial. While eighteen or twenty-four months might not seem light-speed to most people, in the realm of complex federal litigation, cases in the Eastern District are truly on a rocket docket. Similarly, most of the trials described last one week or less. Eastern District rules and practice require the parties to condense difficult matters and explain them to lay jurors in but a few words. Such complex cases in other districts can take weeks or months to try. The likely result is that the jurors oversimplify matters and miss the nuisances of the issues.

This situation, as evidenced by the cases examined above, requires that we consider reforms to correct this broken system of patent litigation. As it stands, the system is unfair and is weighted toward the plaintiffs and trolls seeking to exploit patents that are really just remixes of earlier technology. Our economy depends on innovation, but the specter of Eastern District litigation makes inventors think twice before devoting substantial funds to developing and bringing a new product or process to market.

8

Reformation and the Litigation Explosion

THE PROBLEMS IN the patent litigation arena are reflective of recent trends in the American legal system. As Eric Helland and Alexander Tabarrok have observed in their book *Judge and Jury: American Tort Law on Trial*, "whether we look at expenditures, awards, settlements, or filings, the basic story is consistent: The tort system in the United States expanded significantly during the 1970s and 1980s" so that today we live in an age of a litigation explosion.[1]

What is to be done about the issues surrounding the Eastern District and patent litigation in general? There is no simple answer. However, some combination of the suggestions below could restore some sanity to the system. The problem certainly cannot be ignored. Much of our economy depends on innovation and a court system that provides a neutral playing field where matters can be litigated. Right now, the trolls place a hefty tax on innovative activity and enjoy a significant advantage in court as they push cases into the Eastern District.

Software Patents and Trolls

Scholars note that "problems associated with patent trolling seem to have disproportionally affected the software industry by diverting resources from innovation and weighing down the legal system."[2] Software is different from other industries where manufacturing and development costs counsel in favor of a lengthy period of patent protection. "Software companies have dramatically shorter timelines as the inventions and discoveries made in the software industry have a much shorter lifespan due to the rapid changes in software technology."[3] Because of this short lifespan for products, a twenty-year patent term encourages trolls to purchase older patents for software programs and then to assert that a new program infringes the older patent. Fighting the trolls siphons money away from research and development.

Alexander Tabarrok, a professor at George Mason University, emphasizes that "maximizing innovation requires treating different industries differently."[4] Unlike, say, pharmaceuticals, the software industry does not have high "innovation-to-imitation costs," Tabarrok points out, and thus long patent terms do not promote software innovation, but rather result in stagnation.[5] Rather than twenty years for software patents, the United States should consider a shorter term such as five years. At the end of five years, most software has the value of yesterday's newspapers. This abridged time horizon would allow inventors to reap profits from their work and deny trolls the use of an older patent to shake down new inventors and thus hamper our progress in the information age.

Accounting for Venues

Complaints filed in patent infringement cases predicate venue on 28 U.S.C. § 1400(b). This statute authorizes venue jurisdiction over any patent infringement "in the judicial district where the defendant resides, or where the defendant has committed acts of infringement and has a regular and established place of business."[6] Statutory law further provides that a corporate defendant "reside[s] in any judicial district in which it is subject to personal jurisdiction at the time the action is commenced."[7] Personal jurisdiction typically is established when an entity has certain minimum contacts with the jurisdiction so that due process is not offended if the entity is brought into court. This is a low standard.

For patent cases, there should be a separate statute defining the residence of a corporate defendant. For example, patent defendants might be said to reside in any state where they are incorporated or where they have their principal places of business. Under U.S Supreme Court case law, a principal place of business "refer[s] to the place where a corporation's officers direct, control, and coordinate the corporation's activities."[8] The Court explained that a principal place of business "should normally be the place where the corporation maintains its headquarters—provided that the headquarters is the actual center of direction, control, and coordination, i.e., the 'nerve center.'"[9] Defining residence in this manner in patent cases would considerably cut down on forum shopping.

Making Venue Transfers Easier

Another way to limit forum shopping would be to make it easier for defendants to have a case transferred to another district. Courts typically look at the following factors when entertaining such a motion: (1) the plaintiff's choice of forum, (2) the relative convenience of the parties, (3) the convenience of the witnesses and location of documents, (4) any connection between the forum and the issues, (5) the law to be applied and (6) the state or public interests at stake.[10] Unfortunately, in the Eastern District of Texas, the factors almost always seem to weigh in the plaintiff's favor. A remedy for this would be to place a heavier burden on the plaintiff to show proper venue if the defendant does not have its headquarters in the district of litigation or have a substantial presence there. The plaintiff would have to show by clear and convincing evidence that the suit should go forward in the Eastern District of Texas. Defendants would be more successful if they asked the court to transfer venue to a more appropriate district.

Professional Juries?

The fact that patent plaintiffs covet an uneducated jury unfamiliar with technology shows that a problem exists. It is far too easy for plaintiffs' lawyers to mislead or confuse a jury when presenting evidence in a patent case. The Constitution's Seventh Amendment commands that "in Suits at common law, where the value in controversy shall exceed twenty dollars, the right of trial by jury shall be preserved, and no fact tried by a jury shall be otherwise re-examined in any Court of the United States, than according to the rules of the common law."[11] While the Constitution requires a jury trial in civil cases, such as patent claims, it does not require that a lay jury be used. With patent cases, we should consider a specialized or professional jury to decide the dispute.

For patent trials, courts could require the jurors to possess a formal education in the sciences or technology and in some cases specialized knowledge in the particular field related to the patent. Commentators favoring such a system have noted that "expert juries have had a long history in U.S. and English jurisprudence."[12] In England, for example, trade disputes were often heard by a jury of specialists; this "practice goes back at least to the fourteenth century, and was in use during the centuries immediately preceding the American Revolution."[13] However, commentators also acknowledge that legal challenges might arise if certain groups are not proportionately represented in a specialized jury pool.

Patent attorney Yan Leychkis, after noting that "the United States has the dubious distinction of being the only country in the world which allows lay juries to decide patent cases," argues that not just specialized but professional juries should be considered for patent cases.[14] Leychkis figures that because a patent trial lasts between one week and one month, a "set of twelve jurors and three alternates could decide about twenty cases per year."[15] Because only about a hundred patent cases actually go to trial every year, ten sets of professional jurors could decide all such cases throughout the United States.[16]

Many will no doubt complain that this would be a departure from our well-established citizen jury system. Critics should remember that a strength of the jury system as it developed was that the jurors of the locality had familiarity with the people involved and the subject matter of the dispute. In boundary disputes, the jurors typically knew the lay of the land and the character of the parties to the litigation. This specialized knowledge made local juries the proper and best tribunal to decide the disputes. Modern juries in many cases—especially patent litigation in East Texas—have no knowledge of the subject matter or of the parties. The historic reasons for the development and use of local juries are not present in patent cases.

Specialized Patent Courts?

Just as the Federal Circuit is the designated court of appeals for all patent cases in the United States, Congress should consider creating a specialized patent trial court. Patent law and the underlying technology are extremely complicated. District judges are generalists and lack the background to effectively handle patent litigation. When carrying a full criminal and civil docket, judges have little time to study the complex intricacies that drive patent cases. A district court system where judges have technical background and decide patent matters only would be an improvement over the current system. Leychkis notes that more than "a dozen foreign countries already have this type of specialized trial court."[17] Such a court would sound the death knell of patent forum shopping.

Adjudication and the International Trade Commission

The United States International Trade Commission (ITC), formerly known as the United States Tariff Commission, is an administrative agency that adjudicates intellectual property disputes. The ITC is empowered to investigate claims regarding intellectual property rights, including allegations of patent infringement by imported goods. If infringement occurs, the primary remedy is an exclusion order that directs U.S. Customs officers to stop infringing imports from entering the United States. Scholars note that "in recent years, the ITC has become a forum of choice to litigate patent disputes, particularly in the realm of consumer electronics. This is due in large part to fast adjudication and the availability of the powerful exclusion order. Since substantial manufacturing operations have moved abroad, an ITC exclusion order can swiftly close off the U.S. market to imported products."[18] An administrative law judge presides over an ITC proceeding. The losing party may appeal to the Commission Board of the ITC and seek further appellate recourse at the Court of Appeals for the Federal Circuit.

Because the primary mission of the ITC is to target unfair trade, a complainant must meet the so-called *domestic industry requirement.* To meet this requirement the complainant must show that the patent at issue relates to an industry in the United States that already exists or is in the process of being established. This is done by showing the patent holder (1) has a major investment in plant and equipment, (2) has major employment of workers, or (3) has major investment in the exploitation of the patent.[19]

Congress should consider an industry requirement to bring a patent infringement suit in district court. Rather than the ITC domestic industry requirement, an *international industry* requirement would better fit within a district court setting. So long as a patent holder can show that it is actively participating in an industry that exists or is being established, the doors of the district courts are open. Trolls without plants, equipment, employees, or significant investments in the patents would not be allowed to bring suit. This would not bar the courthouse to legitimate NPEs such as research universities that can show substantial investments in "engineering, research and development, or licensing" related to the patent.[20] But it would make life much more difficult for the trolls.

The industry requirement could impose a burden on individual inventors who have not had a chance to create their new product or to raise substantial amounts for investment. To keep the courthouse accessible to these worthy innovators, it has been suggested that they could post a bond in the absence of an industry affiliation. Tina M. Nguyen explains: "An analogous bond situation exists in corporate law. In corporate law, shareholders can bring derivative suits against the directors of the corporation on behalf of the corporation if they believe that the directors have done something that is detrimental to the corporation as a whole."[21] The posting of a bond to cover the defendant's expenses and attorney fees if an action is unsuccessful would guard against frivolous suits by someone hoping to extort money based solely on the nuisance value of the suit. The courthouse would remain open to viable claims, even if an industry has yet to be established by the creation of a new process or machine.

In the alternative to an industry requirement, patent law could borrow from trademark law and require that a plaintiff prove use. This requirement prevents the warehousing of potentially useful marks. A person or entity may file a trademark application based on an intent to use the mark in commerce. This means that the applicant must have bona fide intention—not a mere bald allegation—to actually use the mark, that is, in fact sell a product to the public with the mark attached. The rights to a trademark can be lost if the holder stops selling the product. A trademark is abandoned when the owner ceases using it. Under the law, nonuse for three consecutive years is prima facie evidence that the holder has abandoned the mark.

Transferring this idea to patent law, a patent defendant could raise the defense of use against a troll. A troll that does not present some evidence of efforts to actually use the patented technology or device in commerce would be deprived of the right to sue. Trolls would undoubtedly try to devise nominal uses of the technology to meet the use requirement, but the courts could evaluate the alleged use and determine if it represents a good faith attempt to practice the invention or is merely a minimal effort meant to open a courthouse door.

Prior to adoption of a use requirement we would also have to consider the risks that individual inventors with little capital might not have the wherewithal to exploit their idea commercially. The rights of such inventors must carefully be balanced against the harm caused by trolls. Perhaps an exception could be created for legitimate inventors who can make a showing that they are not NPEs and that their nonuse is merely a transitory state until they can raise capital or sell/license the patent to an entity who will use the idea.

Learning from the European System

The United States could learn much from Europe in the area of patents and troll control. Unlike the United States, Europe has largely avoided the mischief of the trolls. There are several reasons for this. First, the European Patent Office (EPO) has stricter standards for patentability. Europe does not grant patents for such things as mathematical methods, scientific theories, computer programs, or business methods.[22] These areas are more susceptible to the overbroad or vague claims on which patent trolls thrive.

Using business methods as an example, American companies have patented rather basic methods. Amazon has received a patent for its "1-Click shopping," which permits and encourages consumers to purchase a product by clicking an order button on a webpage. The website stores the customer's billing information and makes online shopping easier for repeat customers. Priceline has patented the "Reverse Auction," which lets users bid on items that are not yet available. Once the item becomes available, the patented system enters the customer's interactive bid.

Prior to 1998, such patents were not allowed. In 1998, the Federal Circuit struck down judicially created exceptions that halted companies from seeking business method patents.[23] Since that ruling, the business method patents have proliferated and enticed sundry trolls. Technically, abstract ideas are still unpatentable, but if one can connect the abstract idea to a new and useful end, then the USPTO will issue a patent. Such a standard leaves the door open for many individuals and NPEs seeking patents for abusive purposes. As we explore ways to restore stability and order to the U.S. patent system, the limitations on patentability that exist in Europe should be considered for adoption in the United States.

The EPO also allows for administrative opposition proceedings to challenge a patent that has been granted. Parties bringing opposition proceedings argue that the patent should never have been granted on the grounds, for example, that the invention lacks novelty or does not involve an inventive step. With the AIA, the USPTO also allows for post-grant reviews, but only for patents resulting from applications filed after March 16, 2013. Some major differences make the EPO proceedings much more effective and efficient. The EPO does not require identification of real parties in interest, and representatives can act in their own name to maintain the anonymity of their clients. This anonymity, which allows a business to challenge a patent without fear of retaliation from the patent holder, is not allowed in USPTO proceedings. Furthermore, initiation of post-grant review proceedings can prohibit a party from raising issues in later proceedings. In Europe, losing the administrative opposition proceedings does not bar later litigation. In the USPTO, the petitioner has the burden of establishing a prima facie case of unpatentability, whereas in the EPO there is a free-ranging evaluation of evidence, which makes it much easier to frame a claim challenging a patent. EPO proceedings are much cheaper than any proceedings in the USPTO. The EPO's administrative proceedings cost about $20,000 whereas USPTO post-grant reviews, according to the experts, will most likely cost $100,000 or more.[24] While the new proceedings authorized by the AIA are a positive step, Congress should look to the European model to make the proceedings more effective.

9

Conclusion

IN THE INFORMATION age, our economy depends on technological innovation. The patent system is supposed to support innovation by granting inventors a temporary monopoly on an invention that they otherwise might be tempted to keep secret. Recent trends in patent litigation are unfortunately discouraging innovation. Patent trolls are using the legal system to ambush entities that actually produce products and employ Americans. In the last two decades, troll lawsuits are responsible for transferring more than half a trillion dollars in wealth to nonperforming entities (NPEs). Trolls and other plaintiffs have found a welcoming atmosphere in the Eastern District of Texas. Court rules, judicial predilections, and favorable jury pools often result in large paydays for the litigious. Rural East Texas is now the national hub of patent litigation. Reform is necessary.

Congress should consider changing the rules for determining corporate residence. For patent cases, residence should hinge on the state of incorporation or the location of the corporate nerve center. The Federal Rules should also make it easier for defendants to challenge venue. Too often litigation is commenced in a district with no real nexus to the parties or the alleged infringement. Plaintiffs should shoulder a heavier burden in defending their choice of forum.

In the same vein, the Federal Circuit should rethink the strict requirement for establishing personal jurisdiction in declaratory judgment actions. Among other things, district courts should be permitted to consider the production of allegedly infringing products in the forum as well as the patentee's sales in the forum. The harsh personal jurisdiction requirements in declaratory judgment actions push more and more litigation to the Eastern District of Texas.

Congress should consider creating a specialized patent court system that uses knowledgeable or professional jurors. Patent matters have become too complicated to trust to generalist judges and lay jurors. A modern patent court system would likely reduce the amount of litigation, discourage trolls, and put innovation—rather than litigation—at the center of the patent system. Finally, Americans should note that Europe does not experience the troll problems that the United States does. European restrictions on what is patentable and the EPO's administrative opposition proceedings should be studied and parts thereof adopted in the United States.

Notes

Chapter 1

1. *See* Paul E. Schaafsma, "An Economic Overview of Patents," *Journal of the Patent and Trademark Office Society,* 79 (1997): 241–44.
2. Quoted in Edward C. Walterscheid, "The Early Evolution of the United States Patent Law: Antecedents (Part I)," *Journal of the Patent and Trademark Office Society,* 76 (1994): 697, 708.
3. Waterscheid, "Early Evolution," 709.
4. Waterscheid, "Early Evolution," 709.
5. Waterscheid, "Early Evolution," 709.
6. An Act concerning Monopolies and Dispensations with Penal Laws . . . , 21 Jac. I, ch 3 (1623).
7. U.S. Constitution, article I, § 8.
8. Joseph Story, *A Familiar Exposition of the Constitution of the United States* (Lake Bluff, IL: Regnery Gatewaym, 1986), 152.
9. Story, *Familiar Exposition,* 152.
10. Story, *Familiar Exposition,* 152.
11. Thomas Jefferson to Isaac McPherson (1813), reprinted in Phillip B. Kurland and Ralph Lerner, eds., *The Founders' Constitution, Vol. 3* (Chicago: University of Chicago Press, 1987), 42.
12. Kurland and Lerner, *Founders',* 42.
13. Kurland and Lerner, *Founders',* 42.
14. 1 Stat 109 (1790).
15. 1 Stat 109 (1790).

16. Michael Kremer, "Patent Buyouts: A Mechanism for Encouraging Innovation," in *Entrepreneurial Economics:Bright Ideas from the Dismal Science,* ed. Alexander Tabarrok (New York: Oxford University Press, 2002), 245.
17. Kremer, "Patent Buyouts," 245.
18. Kremer, "Patent Buyouts," 265.

Chapter 2

1. 35 U.S.C. § 101.
2. Ashley Chuang, "Fixing the Failures of Software Patent Protection: Deterring Patent Trolling by Applying Industry-Specific Patentability Standards," *Southern California Interdisciplinary Law Journal,* 16 (2006): 215, 227.
3. Jeremiah Chan and Matthew Fawcett, "Footsteps of the Patent Troll," *Intellectual Property Bulletin,* 10 (2006): 1, 3.
4. Chuang, "Fixing the Failures," 227.

Chapter 3

1. Peter Detkin, quoted in Anna Mayergoyz, "Lesson from Europe on How to Tame U.S. Patent Trolls," *International Law Journal* (Cornell University), 42 (2009): 241, 245.
2. Victoria E. Luxardo, "Towards a Solution to the Problem of Illegitimate Patent Enforcement Practices in the United States: An Equitable Affirmative Defense of 'Fair Use' in Patent," *Emory International Law Review,* 20 (2006): 791, 796.
3. Chan and Fawcett, "Footsteps of the Patent Troll," 1, 3.
4. Trial Lawyers Inc. Update No. 11, July 2013, www.triallawyersinc.com.
5. Brenda Sandburg, "You May Not Have a Choice," *Trolling for Dollars,* July 30, 2001, www.law.com.
6. 35 U.S.C. § 285.
7. See e.g., *Campbell v. Spectrum Automation,* 601 F.2d 246 (6th Cir. 1979).
8. James Bessen et al., "The Private and Social Costs of Patent Trolls," *Regulation* (Winter 2011–2012): 26.

9. Bessen et al., "Private and Social Costs," 31.

10. Bessen et al., "Private and Social Costs," 31.

11. Bessen et al., "Private and Social Costs," 35.

12. Bessen et al., "Private and Social Costs," 35.

13. Gregory Ferenstein, *Mark Cuban's Awesome Justification for Endowing a Chair to "Eliminate Stupid Patents,"* January 31, 2013, http://techcrunch.com/2013/01/31/mark-cubans-awesome-justification-for-endowing-a-chair-for-eliminating-stupid-patents/.

14. Ferenstein, *Mark Cuban's Awesome Justification,* 2.

15. Ferenstein, *Mark Cuban's Awesome Justification,* 2.

16. Ferenstein, *Mark Cuban's Awesome Justification,* 2.

17. Ferenstein, *Mark Cuban's Awesome Justification,* 2.

18. See "Stragent Foundation Board of Directors," www.stragentfoundation.org.

19. See "About Stragent Foundation," www.stragentfoundation.org.

20. See Jeff Roberts, *How a Texas Dog Park Became a New Front in America's Patent Wars,* October 14, 2011, www.forbes.com/search/?q=texas+dog+park.

21. Roberts, *How a Texas Dog Park.*

22. Roberts, *How a Texas Dog Park*

23. See Mike Masnick, "Why Is a Charity for Abused Kids Suing a Bunch of Tech Companies for Patent Infringement?" *Techdirt,* January 3, 2011, www.techdirt.com/articles/20101230/10555012469/why-is-charity-abused-kids-suing-bunch-tech-companies-patent-infringement.shtml.

24. Trial Lawyers, Update No. 11.

25. Trial Lawyers, Update No. 11.

26. See Trial Lawyers, Update No. 11, for an excellent and more detailed discussion of the Niro and Innovatio's litigation efforts.

Chapter 4

1. 418 F.3d 1282 (Fed. Cir. 2005).

2. See Tina M. Nguyen, "Lowering the Fare: Reducing the Patent Troll's Ability to Tax the System," *Federal Circuit Bar Journal,* 22 (2012): 101, 106.

3. Nguyen, "Lowering the Fare," 107.

4. *NTP*, 418 F.3d at 1289.

5. *NTP*, 418 F.3d at 1290.

6. Michael T. Burr, "Reinventing the Patent Act," *Corporate Legal Times*, October 2005, p. 1.

7. Burr, "Reinventing," 1.

8. Zachary Roth, "Patent Troll Menace," *The Washington Monthly*, June 2005, www.washingtonmonthly.com/features/2005/0506.rothsidebar2 .html.

9. See *Avocent Huntsville, Corp. v. Aten Int'l Co.*, 552 F.3d 1324, 1332 (Fed. Cir. 2008).

10. *Avocent*, 552 F.3d at 1332.

11. The hypothetical used is not hyperbolic but represents the situations that real corporations find themselves in when the trolls attack. See, e.g., *Overstock.com, Inc. v. Furnace Brook, LLC*, 420 F. Supp. 2d 1217 (D. Utah 2005) (holding that patent troll's act of mailing cease and desist letter into the state was not sufficient contact to warrant the exercise of personal jurisdiction.). For an excellent critique of the Federal Circuit's personal jurisdiction jurisprudence, see Marta R. Vanegas, "You Infringed My Patent, Now Wait Until I Sue You: The Federal Circuit's Decision in *Avocent Huntsville Corp. v. Aten International Co.*," *Journal of the Patent and Trademark Office Society*, 92 (2010): 371.

Chapter 5

1. 547 U.S. 388, 391 (2006).

2. For more on the effect of this decision, see Gregory d'Incelli, "Has *Ebay* Spelled the End of Patent Troll Abuses? Paying the Toll: The Rise (and Fall?) of the Patent Troll," *University of Miami Business Law Review*, 17 (2009): 343.

3. Fed. R. Civ. P. 20(b).

4. 35 U.S.C. § 299(a)(1)–(2).

5. 35 U.S.C. § 299(a)(2).

6. See H.R. Rep. 112-98(1), note 61 (stating that "Section 299 legislatively

abrogates the construction of Rule 20(a) adopted in" the Eastern District of Texas).

7. The White House, Fact Sheet: White House Task Force on High-Tech Patent Issues, June 4, 2013, www.whitehouse.gov.

8. Executive Office of the President, Patent Assertion and U.S. Innovation (2013).

9. Executive Office, Patent Assertion.

Chapter 6

1. See James C. Pistorino and Susan J. Crane, "Eastern District of Texas Continues to Lead Until America Invents Act Is Signed," *2011 Trends in Patent Case Filings*, March 2012, www.perkinscoie.com/files/upload/PL _12_03PistorinoArticle.pdf.

2. Pistorino and Crane, "Eastern District," 3.

3. Julie Creswell, "So Small a Town, So Many Patent Suits," *New York Times,* September 24, 2006, www.nytimes.com/2006/09/24/business /24ward.html?pagewanted=all&_r=0.

4. Julie Blackman, Ellen Brickman, and Corinne Brenner, "East Texas Jurors and Patent Litigation," *The Jury Expert* (March 2010), www.the juryexpert.com/2010/03/east-texas-jurors-and-patent-litigation/.

5. Chris Berry et al., *2012 Patent Litigation Study: Litigation Continues to Rise Amid Growing Awareness of Patent Value* 5 (2012).

6. Susan Decker, "A Crackdown on Patently Absurd Lawsuits," *Business-week,* May 10, 2012, www.businessweek.com/articles/2012-05-10/a-crack down-on-patently-absurd-lawsuits.

7. Scalia quoted in Blackman, Brickman, and Brenner, "East Texas Jurors," 6.

8. Berry et al., *2012 Patent Litigation,* 24.

9. Joe Mullin, "Why East Texas Courts Are Back on 'Top' for Patent Law-suits," *Ars Technica,* January 16, 2013, arstechnica.com/tech-policy/2013/01 /east-texas-courts-are-back-on-top-for-patent-lawsuits/.

10. Blackman, Brickman, and Brenner, "East Texas Jurors," 7.

11. Blackman, Brickman, and Brenner, "East Texas Jurors," 7.

12. Blackman, Brickman, and Brenner, "East Texas Jurors," 7.

13. Decker, "A Crackdown," 1.

14. Blackman, Brickman, and Brenner, "East Texas Jurors," 9.

15. Mullin, "Why East Texas," 2.

16. Yan Leychkis, "Of Fire Ants and Claim Construction: An Empirical Study of the Meteoric Rise of the Eastern District of Texas as a Preeminent Forum for Patent Litigation," *Yale Journal of Law and Technology*, 9 (2007): 193, 216.

17. American Tort Reform Foundation (ATRF), *Judicial Hellholes* 27 (2011–12), http://www.judicialhellholes.org/.

18. Leychkis, "Of Fire Ants," 209.

19. Pistorino and Crane, "Eastern District," 9.

20. *Eolas Technologies Inc. v. Adobe Sys., Inc.*, case no. 6:09-446, ECF No. 1.

21. Joe Mullin, "Tim Berners-Lee Takes the Stand to Keep the Web Free," *Wired*, February 7, 2012, www.wired.com/threatlevel/2012/02/tim-berners -lee-patent/.

Chapter 7

1. *Imonex Servs. Inc. v. WH Munzprufer, et al.*, case no. 2:01-cv-174, ECF No 1.

2. *Halliburton Energy Servs. v. Smith Int'l Inc.*, case no. 4:02-cv-269, ECF No 1.

3. *Visto Corp. v. Seven Networks, Inc.*, case no. 2-03-cv-333, ECF No. 1.

4. *Visto v. Seven Networks*, ¶ 6.

5. *TiVo Inc. v. EchoStar Communications Corp., et al.*, case no 2:04-cv-01, ECF No 1.

6. *Paice LLC v. Toyota Motor Corp.*, case no. 2:04-cv-211, ECF No. 1.

7. *z4 Technologies, Inc. v. Microsoft Corp.*, case no. 2:04-cv-335, ECF No. 1.

8. *Finisar Corp. v. DirectTV Group, Inc., et al.*, case no., 1:05-cv-264, ECF No. 1.

9. *Orion IP, LLC v. Mercedes-Benz USA LLC, et al.*, case no. 6:05-cv-322, ECF No 1.

10. *DDR Holdings, LLC v. Hotels.com, et al.*, case no 2:06-cv-42, ECF No. 1.

11. *Mirror Worlds LLC v. Apple Inc.*, case no. 6:08-cv-88, ECF No 1.

12. *Cardsoft Inc. v. Verifone Inc., et al.*, case no. 2:08-cv-98, ECF No 1.

13. *SSL Services, LLC v. Citrix Systems, Inc., et al.*, case no. 2:08-cv-158, ECF No. 1.

14. *SSL v. Citrix,* ¶ 2.

15. See *SSL Services, LLC v. Citrix Systems, Inc.*, 2012 WL 4092449 at *7 (E.D. Tex. 2012).

16. *Fractus, S.A., v. Samsung Electronics. Co., et al.*, case no. 6:09-cv-203, ECF No. 1.

17. Roxanne Palmer, *Samsung Hit for $23M in Fractus Antenna Patent Fight*, May 24, 2011, www.law360.com.

18. *Fractus, S.A., v. Samsung Electronics. Co.*, 876 F. Supp. 2d 802, 851 (E.D. Tex 2012).

19. *Fractus v. Samsung*, 876 F. Supp. 2d at 853.

20. *Cheetah Omni LLC v. Verizon Communications, et al.*, case no. 6:09-cv-260, ECF No. 1.

21. *Soverain Software Corp. v. J.C. Penny Corp, et al.*, case no. 6:09-274, ECF No. 1.

22. *Clear with Computers LLC, v. Hyundai Motor America, Inc.*, case no 6:09-cv-479, ECF No. 1.

23. *Internet Machines LLC v. Alienware Corp., et al.*, case no. 6:10-23, ECF No. 1.

24. *VirnetX Inc. v. Cisco Systems, Inc., et al.*, case no. 6:10-cv-471, ECF No. 1.

Chapter 8

1. Eric Helland and Alexander Tabarrok, *Judge and Jury: American Tort Law on Trial* (Oakland, CA: The Independent Institute, 2006), 7–8.

2. Chuang, "Fixing the Failures," 215, 245.

3. Chuang, "Fixing the Failures," 245–46.

4. Alexander Tabarrok, *Launching the Innovation Renaissance* (New York: Ted Donverence, 2011), 22.

5. Tabarrok, *Launching*, 24.

6. 28 U.S.C. § 1400(b).

7. 28 U.S.C. § 1391(c).

8. *Hertz Corp. v. Friend*, 559 U.S. ___, 130 S.Ct. 1181, 1192 (2010).

9. *Hertz v. Friend*, 130 S.Ct. at 1192.

10. See, e.g., *Momenta Pharm. Inc. v. Amphastar Pharm. Inc.*, 841 F. Supp. 2d 514, 522 (D. Mass. 2012).

11. U.S. Constitution, amend. VII.

12. Michael A. Fisher, "The Legality of Expert Juries in Patent Litigation," *Columbia Science and Technology Law Review,* 2 (2001): 1, 17.

13. Fisher, "The Legality," 18.

14. Leychkis, "Of Fire Ants," 230.

15. Leychkis, "Of Fire Ants," 230.

16. Leychkis, "Of Fire Ants," 230.

17. Leychkis, "Of Fire Ants," 227.

18. Daniel E. Valencia, "Appeals from the International Trade Commission: What Standing Requirement?" *Berkeley Technology Law Journal,* 27 (2012): 1171, 1172.

19. See 19 U.S.C. § 1337(a)(3).

20. 19 U.S.C. § 1337(a)(3)(C).

21. Nguyen, "Lowering the Fare," 130.

22. Mayergoyz, "Lessons from Europe," 258.

23. See *State St. Bank & Trust Co. v. Signature Fin. Group, Inc.*, 149 F.3d 1368 (Fed Cir. 1998).

24. See Steve Seidenberg, "New USTPO Post-Grant Review: A Small Step for Patent Harmonization," *Intellectual Property Watch,* October 2012, www.kilpatricktownsend.com/~/media/Files/articles/2012/IP%20Watch _Oct%202012_post-grant%20review.ashx.

Selected Bibliography

Bender, Gretchen A. "Uncertainty and Unpredictability in Patent Litigation: The Time is Ripe for a Consistent Claim Construction Methodology." *Journal of Intellectual Property Law,* 8 (2001): 175.

Berry, Chris et al., *2012 Patent Litigation Study: Litigation Continues to Rise Amid Growing Awareness of Patent Value* 5 (2012).

Bessen, James et al. "The Private and Social Costs of Patent Trolls." *Regulation* (Winter 2011–2012): 26–35.

Chan, Jeremiah, and Mathew Fawcett. "Footsteps of the Patent Troll." *Intellectual Property Bulletin,* 10 (2006): 1–11.

Chuang, Ashley. "Fixing the Failures of Software Patent Protection: Deterring Patent Trolling by Applying Industry-Specific Patentability Standards." *Southern California Interdisciplinary Law Journal,* 16 (2006): 215–251.

Chuang, Chester S. "Offensive Venue: The Curious Use of Declaratory Judgment to Forum Shop in Patent Litigation." *George Washington Law Review,* 80 (2012): 1065–1114.

d'Incelli, Gregory. "Has *Ebay* Spelled the End of Patent Troll Abuses? Paying the Toll: The Rise (and Fall?) of the Patent Troll." *University of Miami Business Law Review,* 17 (2009): 343–364.

Farnese, Patricia L.. "Patently Unreasonable: Reconsidering the Responsibility of Patentees in Today's Inventive Climate." *Tulane Journal of Technology and Intellectual Property,* 6 (2004): 1–31.

Fisher, Michael A. "The Legality of Expert Juries in Patent Litigation." *Columbia Science and Technology Law Review,* 2 (2001): 81.

Golden, John M. "The Supreme Court as a 'Prime Percolator': A Prescription for Appellate Review of Questions in Patent Law." *UCLA Law Review,* 56 (2009): 657–722.

Helland, Eric, and Alexander T. Tabarrok. *Judge and Jury: American Tort Law on Trial* (Oakland, CA: The Independent Institute, 2006).

Jefferson, Thomas to Isaac McPherson (1813), reprinted in Phillip B. Kurland and Ralph Lerner, eds., *The Founders' Constitution, Vol. 3* (Chicago: University of Chicago Press, 1987), 42.

Klar, Richard B. "*Ebay Inc. v. Mercexchange, L.L.C.*: The Right to Exclude under U.S. Patent Law and the Public Interest." *Journal of the Patent and Trademark Office Society,* 88 (2006): 852–858.

Kurland, Phillip B. and Ralph Lerner, eds. *The Founders' Constitution, Vol. 3* (Chicago: University of Chicago Press, 1987).

Landers, Amy M. *Understanding Patent Law* (New York: NexisLexis Group, 2012).

Leychkis, Yan. "Of Fire Ants and Claim Construction: An Empirical Study of the Meteoric Rise of the Eastern District of Texas as a Preeminent Forum for Patent Litigation." *Yale Journal of Law and Technology,* 9 (2007): 193–233.

Luxardo, Victoria E. "Towards a Solution to the Problem of Illegitimate Patent Enforcement Practices in the United States: An Equitable Affirmative Defense of 'Fair Use' in Patent." *Emory International Law Review,* 20 (2006): 791–831.

Magliocca, Gerard N. "Blackberries and Barnyards: Patent Trolls and the Perils of Innovation." *Notre Dame Law Review,* 82 (2007): 1809–1838.

Mayergoyz, Anna. "Lesson from Europe on How to Tame U.S. Patent Trolls." *International Law Journal* (Cornell Univeristy), 42 (2009): 241–270.

Merges, Robert P. "The Trouble with Trolls: Innovation, Rent-Seeking, and Patent Law Reform." *Berkeley Technology Law Journal,* 24 (2009): 1583–1614.

Moore, Kimberly A. "Forum Shopping in Patent Cases: Does Geographic Choice Affect Innovation?" *North Carolina Law Review,* 79 (2001): 889.

Mueller, Janice. *Patent Law* (New York: Aspen Publishers, 2012).

Nard, Craig A. *The Law of Patents* (New York: Aspen Publishers, 2010).

Nguyen, Tina M. "Lowering the Fare: Reducing the Patent Troll's Ability to Tax the System." *Federal Circuit Bar Journal,* 22 (2012): 101–133.

Rader, Randall R. "The State of Patent Litigation." *Federal Circuit Bar Journal,* 21 (2012): 331–345.

Risch, Michael. "Patent Troll Myths." *Seton Hall Law Review,* 42 (2012): 457–499.

Schaafsma, Paul E. "An Economic Overview of Patents." *Journal of the Patent and Trademark Office Society,* 79 (1997): 241–44.

Schwartz, David L. "Practice Makes Perfect? An Empirical Study of Claim Construction Reversal Rates in Patent Cases." *Michigan Law Review,* 107 (2008): 223–284.

Sichelman, Ted. "Commercializing Patents." *Stanford Law Review,* 62 (2010): 341–411.

Story, Joseph. *A Familiar Exposition of the Constitution of the United States* (Lake Bluff, IL: Regnery Gatewaym, 1986).

Tabarrok, Alexander. *Launching the Innovation Renaissance* (New York: Ted Donverence, 2011).

Tabarrok, Alexander, ed. *Entrepreneurial Economics: Bright Ideas from the Dismal Science* (New York: Oxford University Press for The Independent Institute, 2002).

Valencia, Daniel E. "Appeals from the International Trade Commission: What Standing Requirement?" *Berkeley Technology Law Journal,* 27 (2012): 1171–1199.

Vanegas, Marta R. "You Infringed My Patent, Now Wait Until I Sue You: The Federal Circuit's Decision in *Avocent Huntsville Corp. v. Aten International Co.*" *Journal of the Patent and Trademark Office Society,* 92 (2010): 371–397.

Vishnubhakat, Saurabh. "Reconceiving the Patent Rocket Docket: An Empirical Study of Infringement Litigation 1985–2000," *John Marshall Review of Intellectual Property Law,* 11 (2011): 58–82.

Walterscheid, Edward C. "The Early Evolution of the United States Patent Law: Antecedents (Part I)." *Journal of the Patent and Trademark Office Society,* 76 (1994): 697–715.

Zidel, Andrew T. "Patent Claim Construction in the Trial Courts: A Study Showing the Need for Clear Guidance From the Federal Circuit." *Seton Hall Law Review,* 33 (2003): 711–67.

Index

About the Author

WILLIAM J. WATKINS, JR. is a Research Fellow at the Independent Institute. He received his B.A. in history and German summa cum laude from Clemson University and his J.D. cum laude from the University of South Carolina School of Law. He is a former law clerk to Judge William B. Traxler, Jr. of the U.S. Court of Appeals for the Fourth Circuit, and he has served as Assistant U.S. Attorney, Associate at Womble Carlyle Sandridge & Rice, and Associate with Leatherwood Walker Todd & Mann.

His books include *Judicial Monarchs: The Case for Restoring Popular Sovereignty in the United States* and the Independent Institute book, *Reclaiming the American Revolution: The Kentucky and Virginia Resolutions and Their Legacy* (Palgrave/Macmillan), and his scholarly articles have appeared in the *South Carolina Law Review, The Independent Review, Duke Journal of Constitutional Law and Public Policy, Exploring American History Encyclopedia*, and *America in World History Encyclopedia*.

Mr. Watkins is the recipient of the R. Glen Ayers Award for Historical Writing and the CALI Award for Contracts I, Civil Procedure, Problems in Professional Responsibility. His popular articles have appeared in the *Christian Science Monitor, Forbes, Daily Caller, USA Today, Washington Times, Austin American-Statesman, Providence Journal, San Jose Mercury News, Washington Examiner, Denver Post, Fort Worth Star-Telegram, Bellingham Herald, Lexington Herald-Leader, Sacramento Bee, Duluth News Tribune, Janesville Gazette, Walworth County Today, Wapakoneta Daily News, Dispatch, La Crosse Tribune, Lewiston Sun Journal, Newport Daily News, San Francisco Examiner, Human Events, Chronicles*, and *Silicon Valley/San Jose Business Journal*.

Independent Studies in Political Economy